Nicola Phillipson TEP is a private client barrister at Parklane Plowden Chambers in Leeds whose practice encompasses probate and inheritance disputes, trusts, and property and financial matters in the Court of Protection. Nicola is recognised as a Band 1 ranked barrister in Chambers and Partners and a Tier 1 Leading Junior in the Legal 500.

Nicola is also the author of 'A Practical Guide to the Law in Relation to Control of the Body After Death', published by Law Brief Publishing, considering the law relating to disputes over the body, funerals, graves, and ashes.

A Practical Guide to the Law in Relation to Presumption of Death and Guardianship Orders

A Practical Guide to the Law in Relation to Presumption of Death and Guardianship Orders

Nicola Phillipson TEP

Barrister

Parklane Plowden Chambers, Leeds

MA (Hons) (Oxon) Jurisprudence

Law Brief Publishing

Published 2025 by Law Brief Publishing, an imprint of Law Brief Publishing Ltd
30 The Parks
Minehead
Somerset
TA24 8BT

www.lawbriefpublishing.com

Paperback: 978-1-916698-67-3

In memory of Katie Groves who, as a housing solicitor, never had cause to declare anyone presumed dead, but who was an all-round wonderful human being.

PREFACE

This book covers claims under two Acts, the Presumption of Death Act 2013 and the Guardianship (Missing Persons) Act 2017, and as these are two separate Acts, I have written introductions to each Act before the relevant sections in the book.

My previous book, 'The Law in Relation to Control of the Body After Death', was described recently by a solicitor as one of those books that you have on the shelf that you don't need very often. But then you get a phone call, and you're asked a question, and you reach for the book and the answer is just there.

This description made me very happy and is also the aim of this book. It is another niche book on a subject that doesn't come up that often but will hopefully be very useful when it does. It is a practical textbook designed to give practical assistance when considering and making applications under the Acts, and as such there is a degree of duplication in the chapters.

This book covers the following:

Applications under the Presumption of Death Act 2013

Introduction and the interplay with the Guardianship (Missing Persons) Act 2017

1. The threshold for making an application – considering who can be an applicant, who can be the subject of a declaration and what 'missing' means within the context of the Act.

2. When an application can be made – this chapter looks at the two scenarios in which an application can be made, (i) that a missing person is thought to have died, and (ii) that a missing person has not been known to be alive for a period of at least seven years.

3. The date and time of presumed death – the way the date and time of the presumed death is calculated is different depending upon which of the two scenarios the declaration is based upon, and the result can have very significant consequences.

4. The effect of the declaration and ancillary orders – this chapter considers the effect of a declaration and any subsequent variation or revocation, upon marriages and civil partnerships, property and trusts, and capital sums paid by insurers.

5. How to make the application – the practical part of the book setting out how you issue, what needs to be included in the application, how you must issue without naming a defendant, who needs to be served with the application, how the application must be advertised, and how to apply for relief from sanctions if necessary.

6. Intervenors – who can intervene and how.

7. The first hearing – the first hearing is a case management hearing, but a final order can be made if appropriate.

8. Information from third parties and DWP applications.

9. The final hearing and the order – there are different forms to use depending upon whether you have issued in the Family or Business and Property Courts.

10. Revocation or variation of a declaration – the practicalities of how to make such an application and how to amend Annex A information.

Applications under the Guardianship (Missing Persons) Act 2017

Introduction, the Code of Practice, uses of the Act, and the interplay with the Presumption of Death Act.

11. The threshold for making an application – considering the definition of 'missing' for the purposes of the Act, and jurisdiction and standing to make an application.

12. The criteria to be satisfied to make an order – this chapter looks at the s.3 criteria which need to be proved if an order is to be made. This chapter also considers what happens when two or more guardians are appointed.

13. The terms of the order – considering the scope of the order, the property and/or financial affairs subject to it, the rights and obligations of the guardian, and the duration of the order.

14. Acting as a guardian – considering the concept of best interests within the meaning of the Act, obtaining the guidance or sanction of the court, expenses and records, and the duration of the order.

15. Variation and revocation – this chapter looks at the effect of a variation or revocation order including on third parties who deal with a guardian after an order has been varied or revoked.

16. Applying for an order – the practical part setting out how you issue, what needs to be included in the application, the missing person as the defendant and service upon them, who needs to be given notice of the application, how the application must be advertised, and how to apply for relief from sanctions if necessary.

17. Intervenors – who can be one and how, and how a claimant must respond to any application for permission to intervene.

18. Hearings and the order – unlike under the Presumption of Death Act, there are no prescribed forms for a guardianship order.

19. Applying for a revocation or variation order – the practicalities of how to do so. This chapter also covers how to make other applications under the Act.

20. DWP Orders – what they are and how to make them.

The law and procedure in this book is believed to be accurate and up to date as of 20/11/2024 but practitioners should be aware that changes can be made to the Civil Procedure Rules with very little warning.

Nicola Phillipson
December 2024

CONTENTS

PART ONE

APPLICATIONS UNDER THE PRESUMPTION OF DEATH ACT 2013

Introduction

As the Act itself states, the Presumption of Death Act 2013 ("the Act") is an "Act to make provision in relation to the presumed death of missing persons; and for connected persons". The intention behind the Act was to provide one mechanism whereby a missing person can be declared to be presumed dead, instead of the various procedures which existed previously[1]. These existing procedures have not been abolished, but s.16 is headed "Other determinations about death of missing person" and s.16(1) provides that no declaration which may be applied for under s.1 may be made otherwise than under this Act", indicating that it is intended that this will be the primary method by which the court will declare that a missing person is presumed to have died.

The explanatory notes to the Act state that, based on experience in Scotland and the level of use of existing procedures in England and Wales, it is expected that around 30-40 declarations will be made each year. This relatively low number reflects the reality that although many more people go missing each year, and may be feared dead by those left behind, most decisions to apply for a declaration of presumed death are prompted by a specific practical need, such as the need to deal with

1 The various procedures are listed at paragraph 3 of the explanatory notes to the Act

property or to administer the estate of the Deceased. If it is not clear that a declaration will be made, consideration should be given to making an application under the Guardianship (Missing Persons) Act 2017.

Interplay with the Guardianship (Missing Persons) Act 2017

If it is not certain that a claim for a declaration that a missing person is presumed to have died is likely to succeed, particularly if seven years have not passed since the missing person was last seen, it is possible for a single claim to be issued under which an application is made for a declaration of presumed death, but with an application for a guardianship order be made as an alternative[2]. It should also be noted that if at any time during an application under the Guardianship Act, the court determines that the missing person has not been known to be alive for 7 years, the court may order that the claim continues as if it had been brought under the Presumption of Death Act[3].

---

2 CPR 57.33(2)

3 CPR 57.33(3)

CHAPTER ONE

THRESHOLD FOR MAKING AN APPLICATION

Despite the wording of s.1(2) of the Act which provides that "any person may apply to the High Court for a declaration that the missing person is presumed to be dead.", the Act does not confer a general right upon any person to apply to the court for a declaration that any other person is presumed to be dead. There are criteria that need to be met both in relation to the person making the application, and the missing person in respect of whom a declaration can be sought, and these threshold criteria need to be met before the court can hear the application.

Who can be an Applicant?

Only a person who has "a sufficient interest in the determination of the application" can bring an application for a declaration under the Act[4]. The following people are automatically assumed to have sufficient interest:

The missing person's:

- Spouse
- Civil partner
- Parent

[4] s.1(5)

- Child
- Sibling (of the full or half-blood[5])

It should be immediately apparent that a person's long-term partner and/or cohabitee is not included within the definition of persons with automatic 'sufficient interest'. This omission led to the application in the case of *Re P (Presumption of Death)*[6] being issued in the name of the minor child of the missing person, with the child's mother, the partner and cohabitee of the missing person, acting as the Litigation Friend. Mr Justice Poole noted that "a long-term cohabitee might be as close as anyone to the subject person and it seems unfortunate that D [the Litigation Friend] had to use her son as the claimant in order to ensure that the application would be determined."

It is also noted that other family members such as grandchildren, aunts and uncles, nieces and nephews, and cousins are also not named as persons with automatic interest, and the Act is silent as to the status of step-parents and/or stepchildren. As such, these potential applicants will need to prove that they have sufficient interest.

Sufficient Interest

This is not defined in the Act and the explanatory notes to the Act state that "it is for the court to decide whether any interest is sufficient for the purposes of [s.1]". Reported cases under the Act are not numerous, but those which have dealt with the issue of sufficient interest suggest that this is not a definition to be applied restrictively.

The first thing to remember when considering whether a potential applicant has sufficient interest is that the interest needs to relate to "the

5 s.20(1)

6 [2021] EWHC 3099 (Fam)

determination of the application". It is not necessary that the applicant has a family, or even personal connection to the missing person. In the case of *Reynolds v Saul*[7], the applicant was a solicitor and the personal representative of the estate of Dennis Fullwood, having been appointed as an attorney to act in the administration of the estate on behalf of Madeline Fitzgerald, a relative of Mr Fullwood and a beneficiary of his estate. The missing person in respect of whom the declaration was sought was the co-owner of the property in which Mr Fullwood had lived. Neither the applicant nor Ms Fitzgerald had known Mr Fullwood during his lifetime and they knew nothing of the missing person save that she was the co-owner, on a joint tenancy basis, of the property. The court accepted that the applicant, as the personal representative of Mr Fullwood's estate, had sufficient interest in the determination of the application as the estate "has a real and substantial interest in the question whether [the missing person] is presumed to have died, and when, for the purpose of ascertaining which of them is the survivor of the other and into whose estate [the property] falls."

The court in *Reynolds* was referred to the case of *In re Fisher*[8] in which the applicant was a close friend of the missing person and one of the executors named in a will made by the missing person. In considering whether the applicant had standing to make the application, Judge Paul Matthews noted that family and close friends have emotional interest in each other's lives, some people have a financial interest in the continued lives of others, some have a financial interest in the deaths of others, and the public itself, through aspects of government such as taxation or social security, may have an interest in the missing person. "How far the term 'sufficient interest' in the 2013 Act extends to these various interests, and indeed others, is a matter which should be decided on the usual casuistic basis." The judge stated that the interest of a person in succeeding to the property of another on his death is a well-known interest, and accepted that "a person who intends to prove a testamentary paper *does* have a

7 PT-2024-LDS-000054 (neutral citation awaited)

8 [2023] EWHC 979 (Ch)

sufficient interest in applying for a declaration of presumption of death, even though the paper has not yet been proved."

Who can be the subject of a declaration?

Pursuant to s.1 the missing person must fall into one of these categories:

(i) the missing person was domiciled in England or Wales on the day upon which (s)he was last known to be alive,

(ii) the missing person was habitually resident in England or Wales throughout the period of 1 year, ending with the day upon which (s)he was last known to be alive,

(iii) the applicant is the spouse or civil partner of the missing person and the applicant is domiciled in England or Wales on the day the application is made, or

(iv) the applicant is the spouse or civil partner of the missing person and the applicant has been habitually resident in England or Wales throughout the period of 1 year, ending with the day upon which the application is made.

The concept of domicile is used in the usual common-law sense, and the standard of proof used throughout the Act is the civil standard of balance of probabilities[9]. An examination of the law of domicile is beyond the scope of this book, but the "Commentary on Sections" set out at the conclusion of the Act states at paragraph 15 that the conditions of domicile "require a certain connection with England and Wales" and that "Domicile is the legal concept used to connect a person to a legal jurisdiction, such as England and Wales. It defines where a person is deemed to have his or her permanent home."

---

9 *Greathead v Greathead* [2017] EWHC 1154 (Ch)

The need to satisfy the threshold requirement of domicile must not be forgotten and should be considered at the outset of any case. The application in *Reynolds v Saul*[10] failed as the applicant was unable to prove that the missing person fell into any of the categories above.

An application for a declaration cannot be made in respect of the reigning monarch[11].

Missing Person

It is appropriate at this stage to note that although the person in respect of whom the declaration is sought is described throughout the act as a 'missing person', this is a descriptive term, rather than an independent criterion to be satisfied. This is in contrast to an application under the Guardianship (Missing Persons) Act 2017[12].

The term 'missing person' is defined in s.20(1) of the Act as "the person who is or would be the subject of the declaration".

In *Reynolds v Saul*[13], the subject of the application was Paulene Saul, a person about whom absolutely nothing was known save that she was named as the joint tenant of a flat which was connected to the estate the applicant was administering. All attempts to find any information about Ms Saul had been unsuccessful and the administrator made an application under the Act for a declaration that Ms Saul be presumed to have died seven years after 1 October 1973, the date of the transfer of the property into the joint names of Ms Saul and the deceased. The application failed due to an inability to prove the domicile of Ms Saul, but the court accepted that the applicant did not need to prove that Ms

10 PT-2024-LDS-000054 (neutral citation awaited)

11 s.21(2)

12 See chapter 11

13 PT-2024-LDS-000054 (neutral citation awaited)

Saul was 'missing' in the usual sense of the word, and the fact that the applicant could not prove the existence of Ms Saul beyond her name on the documents relating to the purchase of the property was not a bar to an application under the Act.

CHAPTER TWO

WHEN CAN AN APPLICATION BE MADE UNDER THE ACT?

Having considered the standing of the subject and the applicant to an application for a declaration that a missing person is presumed to be dead, it is now necessary to turn to the circumstances in which that application can be made. There are two different scenarios[14]:

(a) that a missing person is thought to have died,

(b) that a missing person has not been known to be alive for a period of at least 7 years.

Sometimes the circumstances are such that the application will be made in the alternative, but if only one ground is relied upon, this should be made clear on the claim form.

It is necessary to consider at the outset of a case which ground is being relied upon as the different grounds may result in different dates of death which can have very real practical consequences.

Thought to have died

This subsection is used where there is evidence that a person is thought to be deceased. Examples include both where there is positive evidence such as a missing person subsequently being seen on CCTV to have jumped into the sea from a ship leaving their personal effects behind, or where the death is to be inferred from the evidence available such as a

---

14 s.1(1)

person having unexpectedly gone missing, ceasing communication with those who would be expected to hear from them, and there being no evidence of any use of passports, bank accounts or the like.

If the period for which the person has been missing is less than seven years, the court will need to be satisfied that the missing person has in fact died before a declaration can be made, and the standard of proof to be applied is the usual civil standard of the balance of probabilities[15]. In *Re P (Presumption of Death)*[16], the missing person simply disappeared without explanation. Mr Justice Poole said that it was arguable that the evidence proved that the missing person had died, but the court lacked information about the surrounding circumstances at the time the missing person went missing and "a finding that a person has died should only be made on clear evidence of their death". The court therefore preferred to base the declaration upon the missing person not having been known to be alive for a period of at least seven years.

Not been known to be alive for a period of at least seven years

Under this ground there does not need to be evidence that the missing person is dead, or even that it is likely that (s)he has died. As Chief Master Marsh stated in *Re AB*[17], the test under this limb of the Act is not to establish death, but "is to establish the absence of knowledge of the person being alive".

The court has used this section to make a declaration where the evidence was such that it was thought "more than likely" that the missing person has died but because there was no particular incident pointing to death, the declaration was made of the basis that the missing person had not

---

15 *Greathead v Greathead* [2017] EWHC 1154 (Ch)

16 [2021] EWHC 3099 (Fam)

17 [2019] EWHC 2785 (Ch)

been known to be alive for at least 7 years[18], but it has also been used where there is little or no evidence that the missing person has died.

In *EA v NA*[19] the missing person was the husband of the applicant. At the start of their relationship, the missing person had not had leave to remain in the jurisdiction and the court accepted that the applicant had gone to 'considerable lengths' to obtain leave for him to remain, culminating in the missing person receiving his British Passport in December 2009, at which point the missing person left the applicant. By the time of her application in 2017, the applicant had not heard from the missing person for almost 8 years. The applicant gave evidence that at the beginning of 2010 a person who purported to be a relative of the missing person telephoned the applicant and told her that the missing person had died in Iraq, but without providing any further details. The court granted the application on the basis that the missing person had not been known to be alive for seven years, describing the information that the missing person had died as "somewhat circumspect".

In *Austin v Mitchell*[20], Master Shuman referred to *Re AB*[21] and noted that "the court may make findings on circumstantial evidence" and in *Reynolds v Saul*[22], the court said that it would have been prepared to grant the declaration had domicile been proved, notwithstanding that there was no evidence "to even suggest what may have become of [the missing person]" after she signed documents purchasing a property in 1973.

18 *A v H* [2016] EWHC 762 (Fam)

19 [2018] EWHC 583 (Fam)

20 [2020] EWHC 3486 (Ch)

21 [2019] EWHC 2785 (Ch)

22 PT-2024-LDS-000054

CHAPTER THREE

DATE AND TIME OF DEATH

Once the court is satisfied that a declaration should be made, s.2(2) of the Act provides that the court "must include in the declaration a finding as to the date and time of the missing person's death". The mandatory nature of this subsection must not be overlooked, and the likely time and date of death should be considered by an applicant before making an application, as this can have economic consequences such as an estate or dependents being eligible for pension payments or lump sums, but also an estate being liable to repay earnings or pensions paid after the date of the presumed death.

How the date and time of death is calculated depends upon the basis upon which the court has made the declaration.

Satisfied that the missing person has died

If the declaration is made on the basis that the court is satisfied that the missing person has died it will sometimes be possible for the court to also be satisfied as to the approximate time the missing person died. For example, a person seen on a ship's CCTV to have jumped into the Atlantic Ocean at 01.30 in March could sensibly be presumed to have died sometime between 01.30 and 01.40. In these circumstances, although the order itself can record that the missing person be presumed to have died during the period 01.30 to 01.40, for the purposes of the prescribed information, the time 01.40 will be entered in Annex A[23]. This is because s.2(3) provides:

[23] See chapter 9

> (3) Where the court—
>
> (a) is satisfied that the missing person has died, but
>
> (b) is uncertain at which moment during a period the missing person died,
>
> the finding must be that the missing person is presumed to have died at the end of that period.

This section can cause the court some difficulties with Chief Master Marsh in *Re AB*[24] describing the provisions in s.2(2) as "troubling", and saying:

> 10. If the court is satisfied that the missing person has died and the date of death is clear (as in *Greathead*) it will not be difficult to fix a time of death. The position is less straightforward where there is sufficient evidence to support a finding that the missing person has died but little or no basis for determining when it occurred. The Act has fixed on a period of 7 years as the minimum period to enable a declaration to be made where the missing person has not been known to be alive. The date of presumed death, if the court is not satisfied that the missing person has died, is taken to be the end of the 7-year period. This makes good sense. However, if the court is satisfied that the missing person has died, the provisions in section 2(3) must be applied and they may lead to an anomalous result.
>
> 11. Section 2(3) applies because the court is satisfied that the missing person has died but does not know the date and time of death. The way it is put in the Act is that the court is uncertain at which moment "during a period" the missing

24 [2019] EWHC 2785 (Ch)

> person died. However, the Act gives no clue about how "the period" may be established. The court is required to decide upon a period but may commonly have very little to go on other than that the end of the period can be fixed having regard to the fact that the passage of time makes it increasingly likely that the missing person is dead. It is certainly possible, perhaps illogically, for the "period" in the case of section 2(3) to be longer than 7 years where the available evidence shows little more than the passage of time.
>
> 12. This is not merely a theoretical problem because if the missing person has a pension in payment, or was in receipt of benefits, a substantial sum may have been received during the period in which the person was missing and the estate may face a claim for repayment.

And at paragraph 19 it was said

> 19. ….. The words "during a period" seem to me to add nothing. If the court is uncertain at which moment the missing person died, it will often be artificial for the court to reach a conclusion about a date by which uncertainty disappears, even on the balance of probabilities. In this case, the FCO formed the view, based on intelligence that has not been revealed to the court, that AB's death had occurred before June 2010: but there is no way of knowing how that view was reached or how reliable it is. It is one thing in the overall context of this case to accept the FCO's evidence about the likelihood of death, but another to take May 2010 as being the end of the period for the purposes of section 2(2) of the Act.

In the absence of any evidence of an earlier date, Chief Master Marsh held that the appropriate date for the end of the period was the date of the hearing, and the time of death was the time in the hearing when the court confirmed that the declaration would be granted. This was said to be consistent with the court's power to grant a declaration at any time after the date upon which the person went missing, provided there was evidence to prove death, and Chief Master Marsh could see no basis, on the evidence, for the court fixing an earlier time.

In *Johnson v Persons Unknown*[25], the court provided a written judgment "simply to highlight the difficulties with the provisions of section 2 of the 2013 Act previously pointed out by Chief Master Marsh in the case of *CD, re AB*". In *Johnson*, it was critical to establish the date upon which the death was presumed to have taken place, as it affected the succession of the property in which the missing person had lived with his civil partner. The missing person was 70 and suffering from early-stage dementia when he was last seen on the evening of 29th March 2011. He had not been seen or heard of after this date and there was no movement on his bank accounts, but he was also not matched to any bodies found subsequent to his disappearance. Following the missing person's disappearance his pensions continued to be paid into his account, and his partner severed the equity in their jointly owned home in 2016. The missing person's partner died in 2017.

Upon the basis of the circumstantial evidence, the court was satisfied that the missing person had died, and therefore s.2(3) of the Act applied to establishing the date and time of the death. HHJ Paul Matthews, sitting as a Judge of the High Court, stated at paragraph 9,

> Although I am satisfied that Norman has died, I am uncertain as to at what point between the date of his disappearance and the date of the hearing he died. In cases of this kind where vulnerable persons disappear and are not heard of again, there is in the nature of things a greater likelihood of death at an earlier stage than at a later, such that I consider that the probability that Norman died in the last few days before the hearing as extremely remote. But the

---

[25] [2020] EWHC 207 (Ch)

> problem is that I cannot identify a point between the disappearance and the hearing when the balance of probabilities crosses the line.

The judge referred to *Re AB* and agreed with the difficulties identified, noting that whatever date was used, it would make a significant difference, both in relation to the pension payments received by the missing person's estate, and the devolution of the assets in the missing person's estate who had died intestate. HHJ Matthews noted that s.2(3) provides that where the court is uncertain at which moment after their disappearance a missing person died, the finding "must be that the missing person is presumed to have died at the end of that period"[26] and he followed *Re AB* and found that the missing person was presumed to have died at the date and time of his decision, namely 11.30am on 5th February 2020, noting, "I do not regard this as according with common sense. But in my judgment it at least accords with what the law requires of me …"

These decisions in relation to the time of death should be noted, as it will be necessary to mark the time in the hearing when the confirmation of death occurred, as this time will almost certainly be earlier than the end of the hearing.

In circumstances where there is evidence to satisfy the court of a narrower period of likely death, the court has been prepared to perform "temporal gymnastics to work out what that date and time should be"[27], In *Austin* the court accepted that the missing person died "at some stage" on the night he went missing, but chose the time of death as noon the following day to reflect the fact that 'night' does not necessarily end at midnight. In *Re Thomas*[28], the court was satisfied that something happened to the missing person on the morning he went missing, the result of which was

---

26 s.2(3)

27 *Austin v Mitchell* [2020] EWHC 3486 (Ch)

28 [2023] EWHC 1006 (Fam)

that the missing person died although his body had not been found. The court expressed the hope that the death was quick, but for the purposes of the declaration found that the correct date of death was seven days after he went missing[29].

Not Known to be Alive

Establishing the date and time of presumed death is much more straightforward when the declaration is made upon the basis that the missing person has not known to be alive for a period of at least seven years. In these circumstances, s.2(4) provides:

> (4) Where the court—
>
> (a) is satisfied that the missing person has not been known to be alive for a period of at least 7 years, but
>
> (b) is not satisfied that the missing person has died,
>
> the finding must be that the missing person is presumed to have died at the end of the period of 7 years beginning with the day after the day on which he or she was last known to be alive.

Although the calculation of the date and time is straightforward, it should not be forgotten that the calculation should be carried out before any application is made, to ensure that the applicant is aware of any practical or financial issues which may arise from the presumed date of death.

---

29 The judgment does not provide the time of death but in circumstances such as these, midnight of the 7th day would not be an inappropriate time to record in the prescribed information to the order – see *Greathead* [2017] EWHC 1154 (Ch)

CHAPTER FOUR

EFFECT OF THE DECLARATION AND ANCILLARY ORDERS

As noted in the introduction to this book, most applications for a declaration of presumed death are prompted by the need to address a practical issue. In *Re P (Presumption of Death)*[30] it was the death of the missing person's grandmother, leaving a bequest to the missing person, that led to the application. In *Johnson v Persons Unknown*[31], the application was made following the death of the missing person's civil partner which had resulted in uncertainty as to how the property owned by the missing person and his civil partner should pass, and in *A v H*[32] the applicant wished to re-marry.

Once a declaration has been made and the time for any appeal has passed, a copy of the declaration will be sent by the court to the Registrar General for England and Wales and the death will be entered in the Register of Presumed deaths which is linked for search purposes to the registers of deaths maintained under the Births and Deaths Registration Act 1953. Certified copies of entries in the register can be obtained from the Registrar General and such copies will be in effect a certificate of presumed death and can be used to deal with the property and affairs of the missing person as if the missing person had actually died and a death certificate been issued in the usual way. A missing person's estate will

30 [2021] EWHC 3099 (Fam)

31 [2020] EWHC 207 (Ch)

32 [2016] EWHC 762 (Fam)

therefore be distributed either according to their last will, or upon the rules of intestacy.

Pursuant to s.3 of the Act, subject to provisions concerning appeals, a declaration is conclusive of the missing person's death and the time and date of that death. A declaration is effective against all persons and for all purposes, including for the purposes of acquisition of an interest in property, and the ending of a marriage or civil partnership to which the missing person is a party.

It must however be remembered that the declaration made by the court is of presumed death. As such it is inherently revocable should the missing person subsequently re-appear, and the Act expressly provides for the variation or revocation of a declaration[33]. This residual uncertainty is of course unwelcome when the purpose of an application was to allow an applicant to remarry or to settle property disputes. The Act therefore allows the effects of a declaration to be binding, regardless of any subsequent revocation or variation.

Marriage and Civil Partnership

In relation to the ending of a marriage or civil partnership, s.6(2) provides that a 'variation order' (which includes an order revoking a declaration[34]) does not revive a marriage or civil partnership that was brought to an end by virtue of a declaration. Thus the spouse or civil partner of the missing person is free to enter into a further marriage or civil partnership in reliance upon the original declaration.

---

33 See s.5

34 s.5(1)

Property and Trusts

s.4 provides that when making a declaration, the court may determine any question and make such order as it considers reasonable relating to an interest in property arising as a result of the declaration. An obvious example is determining and declaring that the applicant is the sole legal and beneficial owner of a property which was owned by the applicant and the missing person as joint tenants[35]. s.4 further provides that any order made in relation to property interests can direct that the value of any interest so acquired is not to be recoverable by virtue of an order made under s.7(2) (an order made upon variation of a declaration) and can direct that the value of the interest is not to be recoverable in any circumstances, or is not to be recoverable where conditions specified in the order are met.

The provisions of s.4 are clearly useful and should not be forgotten where the purpose of the declaration is to acquire or determine an interest in property. This is particularly important when the provisions of s.7 are considered.

s.6(1) provides that a variation order does not affect an interest in property acquired as a result of a declaration, but the reader is then directed to "see section 7". s.7 states that when making a variation order, the court may determine any question which relates to an interest in property and arises as a result of the variation order. Pursuant to s.7(2), when making a variation order the court must make such further order, if any, as it considers reasonable in relation to any interest in property acquired by the varied order. However, absent exceptional circumstances, the court must not make an order under s.7(2) if the application for a variation order was made more than 5 years after the original declaration was made.

---

35 Such a declaration was granted in the case of *Austin v Mitchell* [2020] EWHC 3486 (Ch)

If the court does make an order under s.7(2), such an order does not affect income accrued in the period between the original declaration and the date of the variation order and does not affect or provide grounds to challenge "a related good faith transaction" or an interest in property acquired under such a transaction[36]. A related good faith transaction is a transaction under which a person acquires an interest in the subject property in good faith and for value, from either the person who acquired the interest as a result of the original declaration, or as a result of subsequent transactions either directly or indirectly from that person. This subsection clearly has parallels to the term "Equity's Darling" commonly referred to in the Chancery court.

If the relevant property is being, or has been administered under a trust, or an insurer has paid a capital sum as a result of the original declaration, when considering what order to make under s.7(2) the court must, as far as practicable, have regard to the principles set out in s.8.

Insurer paid Capital Sum

Where an insurer has paid a capital sum as a result of a declaration that is subsequently revoked or varied, s.8(6) provides that, save for capital sums distributed by way of annuity or other periodical payment, if the facts relating to the variation justify the same, the capital sum or any part of it should be repaid to the insurer. To ensure that this subsection can be enforced, s.14 provides that, before paying a capital sum to a person in reliance upon a declaration, an insurer can require that person to take out an insurance policy in respect of any claim which the insurer may make in the event of a variation order being made.

36 ss.7(5) and (6)

Trust

Where property is being, or has been, administered under a trust, a person who, but for s.6(1) (that a variation order does not affect an interest in property acquired as a result of a declaration) would have an interest in the property by virtue of a variation order, or a person who would have acquired interest from that person, should be entitled to have made over to him:

- the interest in the property or an equivalent interest in property left in hands of trustee, and
- the value of the interest in the property to the extent that such property has already been distributed.

Where a person acquires an entitlement under a trust as a result of a s.7(2) order, s.7(8) provides that the trustee (which includes an executor, administrator or personal representative[37]) is liable to that person for any loss suffered on account of any breach of trust in the administration or distribution of all or part of the property that is the subject of the order. The court may therefore also order the trustee of a trust to take out an insurance policy in respect of any claim which may arise as a result of a s.7(2) order[38]. Pursuant to s.13(3) the premium price of any such policy may be paid from the trust assets. s.7(8) does not apply to the extent that the trustee's liability is restricted under any enactment or provision within the deed regulating the administration of the trust.

[37] s.20(1)

[38] s.13(1)

CHAPTER FIVE

HOW TO MAKE THE APPLICATION

Once you have established that you have standing and the evidence to make the application, and you know what the practical outcome of any declaration is likely to be, you can turn your attention to the practicalities of how to make the application.

Proceedings under the Act must be issued in the High Court in either the Chancery Division (now part of the Business and Property Court) or the Family Division, and the Civil Procedure Rules ("CPR") apply to all applications even if brought in the Family Division, save that the provisions of the Family Procedure Rules 2020 relating to the drawing up and serving or orders apply in place of the CPR in Part 40[39]. Applications must be issued using the Part 8 procedure.

Contents of Claim Form and Written Evidence

Because applications under the Act procced under Part 8, particulars of claim are not required. Instead, a claim is issued by the issue of a Part 8 Claim Form (N208) and the claim form must be accompanied by any written evidence upon which the applicant intends to rely.

The claim form for an application under the Act must state:

(a) that Part 8 of the CPR applies to the application,

39 CPR 57.18

(b) the question the claimant wants the court to decide, or the remedy being sought and the legal basis for the claim to that remedy,

(c) if the claim is being made under an enactment, what that enactment is, and

(d) if the claimant is claiming in a representative capacity, what that capacity is[40].

In addition, CPR 57.19(2) provides that the claim form must also include, or be accompanied by, the following information where known:

(1) *Information about the claimant*

(a) the claimant's name and address;

(b) the relationship of the claimant to the missing person; and

(c) if the claimant is not the missing person's spouse, civil partner, parent, child or sibling, details of the claimant's interest in the determination of the application;

(2) *Information about the missing person*

(a) the missing person's name and surname, and any other names by which the missing person is or has formerly been known;

(b) the missing person's gender;

(c) the missing person's maiden surname (if any);

40 CPR 8.2

(d) the missing person's date and place of birth;

(e) the occupation of the missing person;

(f) the occupation, name and surname of—

(i) the missing person's spouse or civil partner (or late spouse or civil partner if the marriage or civil partnership ended on death);

(ii) where the missing person was under 16 years of age, the missing person's parents;

(g) the missing person's National Insurance number;

(h) the date on which missing person is thought to have died, or on which the missing person was last known have been alive;

(i) on which of the grounds in section 1(4) of the 2013 Act the court is considered to have jurisdiction to entertain the claim;

(j) the usual or last known address of the missing person; and

(k) the name and address of the spouse or civil partner, parents, children or siblings of the missing person (if any, and if not the claimant);

(3) *Information about steps taken to trace the missing person*

(a) details of any enquiries made or other steps taken to trace the missing person or confirm when the missing person was last known to be alive; and

(b) details of the results of such enquiries or other steps;

(4) *Information about the missing person's property*

(a) an estimate of the total value of the assets of the missing person;

(b) details of property owned by the missing person; and

(c) details of the interest of any other person in the missing person's property which it is sought to have determined by the court; and

(5) *Information about advertisement and recipients of notice of the claim*

(a) details of the newspaper in which the claimant proposes to advertise the claim; and

(b) details of the persons to whom the claimant is giving notice of the claim and, where notice is being given to a person under rule 57.20(1)(f), the nature of that person's interest in the claim.

It is common practice for the information required by CPR 8.2 to be included on the claim form itself, and the CPR 57.19(2) information to be included in an accompanying witness statement. Claims under the Act are issued without naming a defendant, and in practice they are rarely opposed, with the result that the hearing is often one sided. For this reason the applicant has a duty to make full disclosure to the court and the court will usually scrutinise the written evidence carefully. It is therefore good practice for the claim form to be accompanied by a witness statement which follows the headings above. This will also prevent delays in the application being granted as there is a risk that witness statements will be returned to the applicant for re-drafting if the judge has 'find' the necessary evidence.

A draft order with Annex A completed[41] should also be attached to the claim form[42]. If the claim has been issued in the Business and Property Courts, Chancery Form CH42 should be used. If the claim has been issued in the Family Court, Standard Order 19.3 should be used[43].

Issued Without Naming a Defendant

As was noted by Judge Matthews in *Greathead v Greathead*[44], an application for a declaration under the Act does not operate between named parties, both of whom will then be bound by the decision, but it operates against the whole world. s.9 and CPR 57.20 provide a list of persons who must be served with notice of the application, and those people have the option to intervene in the application. There is no reference in the Act or the rules to joining a person as a defendant upon issue, and in *Greathead*, the naming of the missing person as the defendant was said to be "neither necessary nor appropriate." The critical point is that notice has to be given to the required persons and "the sensible course for the future is for the claimant not to name any defendant, and the case to be known simply by the name of the claimant and the name of the missing person, such as '[Name], claimant, in the matter of [name of missing person]'."

Judge Matthews also noted that the standard acknowledgement of service served with the Part 8 proceedings is inapt as the opportunity afforded to the person served with the application is to intervene in, rather than defend, the application.

---

41 See chapter 9

42 Chancery Guide 23.25

For Standard Orders used in the family courts see https://www.judiciary.uk/guidance-and-resources/update-to-standard-orders/

44 [2017] EWHC 1154 (Ch)

Persons to be Given Notice (Served with the Claim)

s.9 provides that a person making an application under the Act must send a notice of the application and any other specified information to the persons specified by rules of court. The rules are found at CPR 57.20 which provides that specified persons must be given notice of the claim "by serving a copy of it" upon them. The Act itself refers to "giving notice of the application" and the same heading is used for CPR 57.20. However, the wording of CPR 57 makes it clear that the claim form and accompanying evidence needs to be served upon the specified persons[45] and certificates of service should be filed with the court prior to the first hearing.

The persons to be served with the application are (where not the claimant):

(a) the spouse or civil partner of the missing person;

(b) any parent of the missing person;

(c) any child of the missing person;

(d) any sibling of the missing person;

(e) if there are no persons within sub-paragraphs (a) to (d), the nearest relative of the missing person known to the claimant; and

(f) any other person (including in particular any insurance company) appearing to the claimant to have an interest in the claim.

Although not specifically mentioned, any cohabitee and/or partner of the missing person is an obvious person who will fall into category (f) and

---

45 See also CPR 57.19 which refers to the filing of acknowledgements of service, and service of the claim form out of the jurisdiction

consideration should also be given to pension companies and any person who would be affected under the missing person's will or intestacy.

Once the relevant persons have been identified, the application must be served "within 7 days after the claim is issued"[46]. If any person gives notice of intention to intervene, the court may then direct that they be joined as a claimant or defendant[47].

If there is no person or institution to be served, an application must be made to issue the claim form without service upon any person, and the application must explain why the claimant believes that there is no such person[48]. This application should be made in accordance with CPR 23 before issuing the claim and should be accompanied by a witness statement explaining why there is no person to serve, and a copy of the proposed claim form.

Advertisement of the Claim

Within 7 days of issue of the claim, the claimant must ensure that notice of the claim is published in the prescribed form and "in at least one newspaper circulating in the vicinity of the last known address of the missing person." [49] The prescribed form is set out at paragraph 2.1 of Practice Direction 57B.

At least 5 days before the first hearing, the claimant must file a copy of the page of the newspaper bearing the advertisement and the date upon which it was published.

---

46 CPR 57.20(3)

47 CPR 57.22

48 CPR 57BPD.1.3

49 CPR 57.21

Relief from Sanctions

s.9(3) provides that the court must refuse to hear an application if the requirements of s.9, giving notice to specified persons and advertisement of the claim, have not been met. If either of these conditions have not been met, or have not been met within the required time, it will be necessary for the claimant to apply for relief from sanctions.

CPR 3.1(2)(a) provides that the court may extend or shorten the time for compliance with any rule or practice direction, even if the application for extension is made after the time for compliance has ended. As the first hearing of an application under the Act is a case management hearing, a failure to comply with s.9 need not be fatal to the application for a declaration, but in applying for relief from sanctions the claimant should ensure that the witness statement addresses the *Denton*[50] criteria; (i) the seriousness or significance of the breach, (ii) the reasons why the failure or default occurred, and (iii) all the circumstances of the case.

50 *Denton v TH White* [2014] EWCA Civ 906

CHAPTER SIX

INTERVENING IN AN APPLICATION

As considered in chapter 5, an application under the Act is made without naming a defendant, but pursuant to s.11, there is an automatic right for the missing person's spouse, civil partner, parent, child or sibling (including a half sibling) to intervene in proceedings. Any other person may intervene in proceedings with the permission of the court.

Pursuant to CPR 57.22 and 57BPD.3, the Attorney General, or any person entitled to intervene must first notify the court of their intention to do so as early as possible by filing and serving on the claimant, notice in writing specifying:

(a) the intervener's name and address;

(b) the intervener's relationship to the missing person (where the intervener is not the Attorney General);

(c) the reasons for intervening; and

(d) particulars of any determination or order sought under section 11(4)(b) or (c) of the Act.

A person who wishes to apply for permission to intervene must serve their application on the claimant and must specify

(a) the applicant's relationship to the missing person or other interest in the proceedings;

(b) the reasons for seeking to intervene; and

(c) particulars of any determination or order sought under section 11(4)(b) or (c) of the Act.

The CPR is silent as to any action which should be taken by the claimant if served with an application for permission to intervene. It is suggested however that it would be prudent to adopt the procedure laid out for Guardianship Orders, under which if the claimant receives an application to intervene from a person who has not been sent the claim form, the claimant must, within 7 days, send the proposed intervenor a copy of the claim form, evidence in support, and notice of the hearing date, and must file with the court and send to the proposed intervenor, a statement setting out whether they object, and any evidence in support of their objection[51]. Such action would ensure that the application can be dealt with at the case management hearing.

If permission to intervene is granted, this may be subject to conditions and upon granting permission, the court may give case management directions.

The court may direct that a person intervening be added to the proceedings as a claimant or as a defendant[52].

---

51 CPR 57.31

52 CPR 57.22

CHAPTER SEVEN

FIRST HEARING

Paragraph 1.4 of PD 57B provides that a claim for a declaration must be listed for a case management hearing more than 28 days, but where practicable no more than 56 days, after issue. The timing allows those served with the claim or who respond to the advertisement to file notice of intention to intervene, or permission to intervene, and the purpose of the case management hearing is for the court to satisfy itself that all the requirements of the Act and the relevant CPR have been complied with, and to give directions as to matters connected to any intervention such as the filing and service of evidence.

However, notwithstanding the mandatory 'must' used in paragraph 1.4, where all the requisite steps have been taken by the claimant and the formalities complied with, the parties served with the application have either not responded or have indicated that they do not wish to intervene in the proceedings, and all relevant persons were aware of the date of the hearing, the application can be heard at the first hearing. This was the situation in *In re Irish*[53] where HHJ Matthews sitting as a High Court Judge exercised his case management powers under CPR 3.1(2)(b)[54] and (m)[55] at the case management hearing to proceed immediately to hear and dispose of the substantive claim, granting the declaration sought.

If the matter is not ready to proceed, and this will often be the case if enough notice was not given of the hearing due to the late service of the application or advertisement, the court will proceed to give directions to

53 [2019] EWHC 2508 (Ch)

54 Adjourn or bring forward a hearing

55 Take any other step or make any other order for the purpose of managing the case and furthering the overriding objective

a final hearing. This is also an opportunity for the court or the parties to identify any deficiencies in the evidence so that the attempts can be made to remedy the same before the final hearing.

Consideration should be given at this hearing to requesting or confirming that the final hearing be dealt with on submissions only.

CHAPTER EIGHT

INFORMATION FROM THIRD PARTIES

s.12 provides that in proceedings for a declaration under the Act, if it is considered necessary for the purpose of disposing of the proceedings, the court may at any stage require a person who is not a party to the proceedings to provide it with specified information that it considers relevant to the question of whether the missing person is alive or dead. Such an order may not require the provision of information which can be withheld on grounds of public interest immunity, legal professional privilege, or incrimination of a person or their spouse or civil partner in an offence[56].

DWP Orders

Practice Direction 6C of the Family Procedure Rules is entitled "Disclosure of Addresses by Government Departments" and applies when the court makes an order, having the power to do so, or makes a request for the purposes of tracing the address of a party or prospective party to family proceedings. The practice direction sets out the information required to be sent to the government department when an order is made by the High Court for the current address of the person named in the order.

---

[56] See *Re AB* [2019] EWHC 2785 (Ch) for a case where the information provided to the court by the Foreign and Commonwealth Office as to the death of the missing person was limited on the grounds of national security

It is clear from practice direction 6C and standard order 3.3[57] that the High Court has inherent jurisdiction to order a government department to disclose the current or last known address of a specified person to the court. This could be of assistance if a person who has been missing for a long time is thought to have had contact with a government department (e.g. had a driving license, paid tax, or was in receipt of state benefits, or payments such as child benefit or a state pension).

An application for a disclosure order against a government department should be made by application at the time the claim is issued, and the order sought can be for disclosure to the court only, or to the applicant's solicitor, upon undertakings by the solicitor not to disclose the information or use it for any purpose other than that specified in the order[58].

The CPR does not have a similar practice direction so applications which are likely to be accompanied by a disclosure application can either be issued in the Family Division of the High Court, or the Family Court standard order can be adapted, the applicant having relied upon the inherent jurisdiction of the High Court to make the application.

---

57 Standard order used in the family courts see https://www.judiciary.uk/guidance-and-resources/update-to-standard-orders/

58 See Standard Order 3.3

CHAPTER NINE

FINAL HEARING

The matters the applicant needs to satisfy to obtain a declaration have already been considered. As applications are not usually opposed and are often dealt with on submissions only, it is clearly important that the witness statements supporting the application should cover all the relevant information and all required documents should be annexed. A draft order should be prepared and skeleton arguments filed with the court in advance.

The Order

If the Business and Property court grants the application and makes the declaration, the order should follow Chancery Form CH42. If the claim has been issued in the Family Court, Standard Order 19.3 should be used[59].

Both forms contain 'Annex A – Schedule of Prescribed Information for the GRO'. This

does not appear upon the final order but is necessary to enable the death to be entered into the Register and should therefore be completed as fully as possible.

As previously considered, pursuant to s.2, when the court makes a declaration, it must include in the declaration a finding as to the date and time of the missing person's death. Where the court is satisfied that a

---

For Standard Orders used in the family courts see https://www.judiciary.uk/guidance-and-resources/update-to-standard-orders/

missing person has died, but is uncertain as to the precise moment within a period that death occurred, the finding must be that the missing person is presumed to have died at the end of that period. I have had cases where the court has found that the missing person died within a specified period and has chosen to specify the period within the body of the order and enter the end of the period in the Annex A information. For example, the Order would state "It is declared that Joe Bloggs be presumed to have died on 4th September 1999 during the period 1.30pm to 2.30pm" and the time entered in Annex A is 2.30pm.

Once a declaration is made, the court must send a copy of the declaration to the Public Guardian[60].

[60] CPR 57.24

CHAPTER TEN

REVOCATION OR VARIATION OF A DECLARATION

As noted by Mr Justice Moor in *Re Thomas*[61], "if, by any chance, [the missing person] was ever to reappear, then, of course, an application could be made to set my order aside."

s.5 provides:

> **5 Varying and revoking declaration**
>
> (1) On an application by any person, a declaration under this Act may be varied or revoked by an order of the High Court (a "variation order").
>
> (2) The court must refuse to hear an application for a variation order if it considers that the applicant does not have a sufficient interest in the determination of the application.

As can be seen from s.5, just as with standing to apply for a declaration, a person wishing to apply for a variation order (which includes an application to revoke a declaration) must have a sufficient interest in the determination of the application[62].

Although not stated in terms in the Act itself, CPR 57 which governs the making of orders and declarations under the Act, makes it clear at 57.19 that an application for a variation order is not made by issuing an

---

61 [2023] EWHC 1006 (Fam)

62 See chapter 1

application within the original proceedings, but is a new originating process, requiring fresh proceedings in the High Court.

The procedure for applying for a variation order also largely mirrors that of an application for a declaration. Readers are therefore referred to chapter 5 for further detail.

The application is made by issuing a claim form in accordance with Part 8[63] which must state:

(a) that Part 8 of the CPR applies to the application,

(b) the question the claimant wants the court to decide, or the remedy being sought and the legal basis for the claim to that remedy,

(c) if the claim is being made under an enactment, what that enactment is, and

(d) if the claimant is claiming in a representative capacity, what that capacity is[64].

In addition, paragraph 1.2 of CPR 57BPD.1 provides that the claim form for a variation order must also include, or be accompanied by, the following information where known:

(1) *Information about the claimant*

(a) the claimant's name and address;

(b) the relationship of the claimant to the missing person; and

---

63 CPR 57.19

64 CPR 8.2

(c) details of the claimant's interest in the determination of the application;

(2) *Information about previous claim and missing person's property*

(a) details of the declaration of presumed death or (as the case may be) previous variation order which it is sought to have varied or revoked;

(b) details of the circumstances which are claimed to justify a variation order, and evidence of the enquiries made and other steps taken to verify them and their outcomes; and

(c) details of any interest in property acquired as a result of the declaration of presumed death or (as the case may be) previous variation order which it is sought to have varied or revoked; and

(3) *Information about advertisement and recipients of notice of the claim*

(a) details of the newspaper in which the claimant proposes to advertise the claim; and

(b) details of the persons to whom the claimant is giving notice of the claim and, where notice is being given to a person under rule 57.20(2)(g)[65], the nature of that person's interest in the claim.

65 Any other person appearing to the claimant to have an interest in the claim

The application is issued without naming a defendant, but the applicant must give notice of the claim for a variation order by serving a copy of it on the following persons (where not the claimant):

(a) the person who was the claimant for the declaration of presumed death or (as the case may be) previous variation order which it is sought to have varied or revoked;

(b) the spouse or civil partner of the missing person;

(c) any parent of the missing person;

(d) any child of the missing person;

(e) any sibling of the missing person;

(f) if there are no persons within sub-paragraphs (b) to (e), the nearest relative of the missing person known to the claimant; and

(g) any other person (including in particular any insurance company) appearing to the claimant to have an interest in the claim[66].

Notice must be given within 7 days after the claim is issued[67].

The application must, within 7 days of issue of the claim, be advertised in the prescribed form in at least one newspaper circulating in the vicinity of the last known address of the missing person., and at least 5 days before the first hearing, the Claimant must file a copy of the page of the

66 CPR 57.20(2)

67 CPR 57.20(3)

newspaper bearing the advertisement and the date upon which it was published[68].

The rules relating to issuing without naming a Defendant and intervening are as for an application for a declaration and are covered in chapters 5 and 6.

The Hearing

The procedure for the listing and hearing of a variation order follows that of an application for a declaration, and the provisions relating to orders for information from third parties is also the same. Readers are therefore directed to chapters 7 and 8.

Effect of a Variation Order

The effects of an order varying or revoking a declaration are covered in chapter 4.

Amendment of Annex A information

In the second *In re Irish*[69] the court was being asked to make an amendment not to the declaration itself, but to the information provided at Annex A of CH42, as the missing person's date of birth had been incorrectly stated both in the original claim and on the Annex A to the order. HHJ Matthews emphasised that this mistake made no difference to the validity of the order making the declaration of presumed death and expressed disappointment that various financial institutions holding assets to be collected in for the administration of the missing person's

68 CPR 57.21

69 [2020] EWHC 456 (Ch)

estate had insisted upon a correction being made to the annex to the order.

The question for the court in *In re Irish* number two was how the court could make such an amendment. Consideration was given to the slip rule jurisdiction, CPR 3.1(7) (the power to vary or revoke any order), and the ability to apply for a variation order under the Act, but the conclusion reached was that the court could make the order under paragraph 5(2) of Schedule 1 of the Act which states:

> (2) Where it appears to the court that there is an error in the Register of Presumed Deaths, the court may direct the Registrar General to secure that the error is corrected.

HHJ Matthews also held that there was nothing in the Act, rules, or practice directions to require the application to be made by a new originating process (unlike for an application for a variation order) and therefore such an application could be made by application in form N244 in the original proceedings.

PART TWO

GUARDIANSHIP ORDERS

Introduction

The Guardianship (Missing Persons) Act 2017 ("the Act") came into on 31 July 2019. Informally known as 'Claudia's Law' after Claudia Lawrence who disappeared in 2009, the purpose of the Act is to empower the court to appoint a guardian to deal with the property and financial affairs of people who have gone missing until either the missing person reappears, or steps are taken to apply for a declaration of presumed death.

The Code of Practice

Guidance for guardians and persons making applications under the Act is provided by the Guardianship (Missing Persons) Act 2017 Code of Practice ("the Code"), the most recent edition of which is dated June 2019.

Paragraph 2.4 of the Code provides:

The guardianship Code of Practice is statutory. The Act provides that guardians must have regard to it; and, in any court or tribunal case where compliance with the Code may be relevant, the court or tribunal must take the Code into account.

It is therefore a document which should be downloaded and consulted if an application under the Act is envisaged.

Uses of the Act and Reported Cases

At the time of writing this book I cannot find any reported cases under the Guardianship Act. I have obtained two orders, but they were both unopposed and neither resulted in a formally handed down judgment which could be reported, which I suspect will be the case for most orders.

The Code provides examples of when the Act can be used – where a person has been kidnapped or imprisoned abroad and cannot communicate decisions to the outside world, or when a person has simply disappeared, their whereabouts are completely unknown, but there is no evidence that they have died, and the requisite seven years for a claim under the Presumption of Death Act 2013 has not yet passed. But the Act can also be used where a person has, for whatever reason, decided to leave their old life behind and move to a place or places unknown, without telling anyone or leaving a forwarding address or means of contact. The fact that they are alive, and their basic location may be known (for example, somewhere in the USA), but if they are refusing to make contact with friends or family left behind, and there is property or financial affairs which need to be dealt with, the Act can be used to obtain an order for this purpose. An order under the Act can also be the solution to a problem such as a building falling into disrepair and causing problems for neighbouring properties. If the owner herself cannot be found, but her relatives can, an order can be applied for to enable the property to be dealt with.

Interplay with the Presumption of Death Act 2013

If it is not certain that a claim for a declaration that a missing person is presumed to have died is likely to succeed, particularly if seven years have not passed since the missing person was last seen, it is possible for a single claim to be issued under which an application is made for a declaration of presumed death, but with an application for a guardianship order be made as an alternative[70]. It should also be noted that if at any time during an application under the Guardianship Act, the court determines that the missing person has not been known to be alive for 7 years, the court may order that the claim continues as if it had been brought under the Presumption of Death Act[71].

70 CPR 57.33(2)

71 CPR 57.33(3)

CHAPTER ELEVEN

THRESHOLD FOR MAKING AN APPLICATION

Missing

The first thing to note in relation to applications under the Act is that before an order can be made, the applicant needs to be able to prove that the missing person is "missing" as defined by s.1 of the Act.

For the purposes of the Act a person is "missing" if they are absent from their usual place of residence, are absent from their usual day to day activities, and one of the following conditions are met:

(i) their whereabouts are either not known at all, or are not known with sufficient precision to enable the person to be contacted for the purposes of decisions relating to their property and financial affairs, or

(ii) they are unable to make decisions relating to their property and financial affairs or to communicate such decisions with a view to their implementation, or both, and the reason for this is something beyond the person's control other than illness, injury, or lack of capacity as defined by the Mental Capacity Act 2005.

s.1(4) provides that a person who is detained, either in a prison or elsewhere, is to be treated for the purposes of the Act as absent from their usual place of residence and day to day activities.

It can be seen from the above that the Act envisages two scenarios in which a person can be said to be missing. The first is said to be a typical scenario for a case under the Act "where a person has simply disappeared without explanation"[72] and is absent from both their usual residence and activities and their whereabouts are unknown or not known precisely enough for contact to be made to obtain decisions.

The second scenario is where the missing person is again absent from both their usual residence and activities and, for reasons beyond the missing person's control, they are unable to make or communicate decisions, or both. The examples given in the Code of Guidance of this second scenario are where the missing person is a hostage or kidnap victim, or where a person is imprisoned abroad in circumstances where they cannot communicate their wishes or deal with their affairs.

s.1(3)(b) makes it clear that a person who lacks capacity, or who is in hospital and unable to communicate their decisions due to illness or treatment, is not 'missing' for the purposes of the Act. Other jurisdictions, such as an application to the Court of Protection, will need to be used to safeguard the property and financial interests of such persons.

Jurisdiction and Standing

Domicile/Habitual Residence

Under s.2 of the Act, the court only has jurisdiction to hear and determine an application for an order if either:

- the missing person was
  - domiciled in England and Wales on the day before they were first known to be missing, or

[72] Paragraph 4.4 of the Code

- had been habitually resident in England and Wales throughout the period of one year ending on the day before they were first known to be missing,

Or

- the application is made by the missing person's spouse or civil partner and the applicant is:

  - domiciled in England and Wales on the day on which the application is made, or

  - has been habitually resident in England and Wales throughout the period of one year ending on the day on which the application is made.

If a person is missing for two or more separate periods, the reference to "day before" is referable to the latest period.

The Code states that domicile is a common law concept used to connect a person to a legal jurisdiction, and defines where a person is deemed to have his or her permanent home[73], which commentary mirrors that of the explanatory notes to the Presumption of Death Act.

Sufficient Interest

s.19 provides that the court must refuse to hear an application for an order unless the applicant has a sufficient interest in relation to the missing person's property or financial affairs.

The following are to be treated as having a sufficient interest:

---

[73] Paragraph 5.5

The missing person's:

- spouse,
- civil partner,
- parent,
- child,
- sibling (including half sibling[74]), or
- a person who was the guardian in respect of some or all of the missing person's property and financial affairs at any time during the period of one year ending with the day upon which the application is made[75].

The Act does not make reference to the criteria by which sufficient interest for persons not specified in the Act is to be judged, but the Code states that the sufficiency of any interest will be case specific[76] and may vary depending on the remedy being sought, with the more significant the remedy, the greater the interest is likely to be. The obvious category missing from those with automatic interests is a long term partner and/or cohabitee, but it should be remembered that the interest needs to be in relation to the missing person's property or financial affairs, not merely an interest in the missing person themselves. The Code makes it clear that non family members could be considered to have sufficient interest, citing hypothetical examples of a business partner and a next door

[74] s.24

[75] Under s.7, the maximum duration of a guardianship order is 4 years, but an application can be made for a further order, including the re-appointment of a guardian

[76] Paragraph 4.22

neighbour with a history of caring for the missing person and assisting with their finances.

CHAPTER TWELVE

CRITERIA TO BE SATISFIED TO MAKE AN ORDER

Under s.3 of the Act, the court can make an order if it is satisfied that:

(i) the missing person is missing,

(ii) either, the missing person has been missing throughout the period of 90 days ending with the day on which the application was made, ("the absence condition"), or

(iii) the absence condition is not met but a decision is needed, or likely to be needed, in relation to the property or financial affairs of the missing person before the day upon which the absence condition would be met ("the urgency condition"),

(iv) in all the circumstances the appointment of a guardian is in the missing person's best interests, and

(v) there is a person who can be appointed as guardian.

(i) The missing person is 'missing'

As examined in chapter 11, the missing person has to be missing within the definition of the Act at s.1, and this will have to be proved by evidence.

(ii) and (iii) Absence or Urgency Conditions

The usual period of 90 days absence can be waived by the court when it is satisfied that there is an urgent decision which needs to be made. Examples given in the Code are an urgent business decision or a repossession claim which the guardian wishes to challenge.

(iv) Best Interests

s.18 of the Act provides that when determining what is in the missing person's best interests, the court or guardian must consider all the relevant circumstances of which the court or guardian is aware, and must consider, so far as is reasonably ascertainable, any relevant wishes and feelings expressed by the missing person at any time, including any written statement, the beliefs and values that would be likely to influence the missing person, and any other factors that the missing person would be likely to consider.

Where it is reasonably practicable and appropriate to do so, the court or guardian must take into account the views of any persons of whom the court or guardian is aware with a relevant interest in relation to the missing person's property or financial affairs. The consequences of taking a proposed action must also be considered. However, the court or guardian is not required to decide any matter by reference to the decision the missing person is likely to have taken, or to consider whether or when the missing person might cease to be missing. In relation to this last issue, it is noted that a missing person may cease to be missing within the context of the Act either because they are found, or because circumstances or the passage of time means that it is appropriate for a declaration of presumed death to be made under the Presumption of Death Act 2013.

If it would be reasonable to expect the missing person to consult a particular person before making a decision, the guardian must consult that person unless it is not reasonably practicable to do so[77]. This could presumably be either a professional such as an accountant or a lawyer, or simply a third party who may have a connection to the issue in question, but who does not fulfil the criteria of having a relevant interest in the missing person's property or financial affairs.

It is expressly stated in the Code that a best interests decision under the Act is to be assessed in light of the provisions of the Act, and it cannot be assumed that the outcome will be the same as a best interests decision made under a different statute, for example the Mental Capacity Act 2005.

(v) Person who can be Appointed

The criteria of eligibility to be appointed as a guardian is set out at s.4 which provides that a person may only be appointed as a guardian if the court is satisfied that the person:

(i) is an individual aged at least 18, or a trust corporation,

(ii) consents to the appointment,

(iii) is suitable to act, and

(iv) will act in the missing person's best interests

In relation to requirement that the court be satisfied that the proposed guardian is suitable to act, it would be appropriate when making the application to file evidence as to the fitness to act of the proposed guardian(s) from an independent person of good standing, as would be filed for a proposed replacement personal representative.

[77] s.8(3)

When considering whether the proposed person is suitable to act, the court must have regard to

(i) the proposed guardian's relationship with the missing person,

(ii) the missing person's views on the proposed guardian so far as they are known to or reasonably ascertained by the court,

(iii) whether the proposed guardian has the skills and knowledge necessary to carry out the functions proposed to be conferred upon them, and

(iv) any conflict between the interests of the proposed guardian and the missing person.

For the purposes of determining whether there is a conflict, the court must, among other things, consider any connection between the property and financial affairs of the missing person and the proposed guardian, and how any such connection might affect the taking of decisions by the proposed guardian. There is not a conflict merely because the proposed guardian is the missing person's spouse, civil partner, parent, child, sibling, or other relative, or because the proposed guardian was living with the missing person immediately before they went missing, or because the proposed guardian may benefit, directly or indirectly, from being appointed.

s.4(5) provides that the court may appoint a person as a guardian "whether or not the person is proposed in the application for the order". This allows the identity of the guardian to change as the application progresses, particularly if the court indicates that it is unhappy with the proposed guardian, or feels that there needs to be an independent professional involved, perhaps as a second guardian.

Two or More Guardians

Pursuant to s.16, the Court may appoint two or more guardians, and these appointments can be at the same or different times, by the means of the same guardianship order, or separate guardianship orders, and the court can make such an appointment whether or not the appointment of two or more guardians is proposed in the application before the court. Different guardians can be appointed for different periods[78].

The Schedule to the Act makes further provision about the appointment of two or more guardians. When appointing two or more guardians, the court must:

(a) provide for them to act jointly,

(b) provide for each guardian to have sole responsibility for specified parts, or

(c) provide for a combination of joint and sole responsibilities.

If the guardians are appointed to act jointly, they must act unanimously, and any directions, conditions, or restrictions imposed by the court applies to each of the guardians. This provision should be remembered if there is an application to appoint an additional guardian after an order has already been made. If they are to act jointly, the additional guardian will be automatically subject to any directions already in place, and any additional direction, conditions, or restrictions will also bind the existing guardian.

The court's power under s.12 to vary a guardianship order includes a power to remove one or more guardian without replacing them, but not to remove all the guardians without replacing any of them.

---

78 Schedule to the Act paragraph 1(5)

If one of the guardians dies, the order is not revoked unless no other guardian remains alive, or the only other guardian alive is appointed only to act jointly with the deceased guardian. If the order is not revoked, the remaining guardian(s) must apply to the court for the variation or revocation of the order as soon as practicable after becoming aware of the death.

CHAPTER THIRTEEN

TERMS OF THE ORDER

A guardian is to be treated as the missing person's agent, with authority conferred by the order and the Act[79]. It is therefore important that the proposed terms of the order are carefully drafted to ensure that the guardian has the necessary authority to make the decisions required.

Property and/or Financial Affairs subject to the Order

Pursuant to s.2(1) the court can make an order in respect of "some or all of a missing person's property and financial affairs" and s.5 provides that an order must appoint the guardian in relation to all of the missing person's property and financial affairs, or the property and financial affairs specified or described in the order.

An order can be made in respect of any property or financial affairs of the missing person, whether or not mentioned in the application, but an order can only be made in respect of property or financial affairs in respect of which the court is satisfied that an order is in the missing person's best interests, and that there is a person who could be appointed as guardian for that property or financial affair.

If the application is made in reliance upon the urgency condition[80], the court can only make an order in respect of property or financial affairs in respect of which it is satisfied that the urgency requirement is met. It can therefore be seen that the situation may arise whereby a very limited order is made on the urgency basis, enabling a guardian to deal only with one

79 s.8(2)

80 See chapter 12 for the urgency and absence conditions

very specific issue, which cannot wait (for example a repossession hearing), and an order is then made at a later date on the absence condition which gives a guardian (either the same or a different guardian) more general powers to deal with the missing person's other property and/or financial affairs.

It can be seen from the above that the court needs to be satisfied, not only that it is in the missing person's best interests to make an order generally, but also that the s.3 factors[81] are satisfied in respect of the property and/or financial affairs which are to be the subject of the application. It is therefore necessary to ensure that an application for an order sets out precisely what property and/or financial affairs are intended to be covered by the order, the reasons why this is in the missing person's best interest, and why the proposed guardian is suitable to deal with this particular property and/or financial affair.

A guardianship order may not relate to the property and financial affairs of more than one person[82], although there would seem to be no reason why the same guardian(s) could not be appointed to deal with the affairs of more than one person.

The Rights and Obligations of the Guardian

A guardianship order does not affect the rights, powers, or interests of third parties in relation to the missing person's property and/or financial affairs[83], and a guardian may not execute a will for a missing person, or exercise a power vested in the missing person as a trustee in relation to another person's property[84].

---

81 Considered in chapter 12

82 s.5(2)

83 s.8(4)

84 s.6(6)

Save as aforesaid, in relation to the property and/or financial affairs covered by an order, s.6 provides that the court must appoint the guardian to exercise all the missing person's rights and powers in relation to the same, or such of those rights and powers as are described or specified in the order.

These rights and powers include:

(a) selling, letting, or mortgaging the missing person's property;

(b) making investments;

(c) executing deeds and other documents;

(d) recovering money owed to the missing person;

(e) discharging debts and other obligations of the missing person (whether legally enforceable or not);

(f) resigning trusteeships held by the missing person;

(g) bringing or conducting legal proceedings; and/or

(h) making a gift out of the missing person's property.

It should however be noted that unless a gift is to be made for the maintenance or benefit of a dependent of the missing person, gifts can only be made by a guardian if authorised by the order. Care must therefore be taken to ensure that an order covers any specific gift(s) intended to be made by the guardian. Unless the terms of the order provide otherwise, a gift to a dependent does not require specific authorisation but is subject only to the best interests test[85].

---

85 The Code, paragraph 5.67

The order can impose duties upon a guardian and can include conditions and restrictions. In particular, an order can require the guardian to give the Public Guardian security for the exercise of the guardian's functions, and require the guardian to submit reports to the Public Guardian at specified times or intervals[86].

Duration of the Order

A guardian is appointed for the period specified in the order, and there is a maximum period of four years beginning with the day upon which the order was made. The court can, however, make a further order in respect of some or all of the missing person's property and/or financial affairs, including an order re-appointing a person as a guardian[87].

For the situation where there is more than one guardian is appointed, see chapter 12, and for revocation of an order see chapter 15.

86 s.6

87 s.7

CHAPTER FOURTEEN

ACTING AS A GUARDIAN

Best Interests

A guardian must act in what they reasonably believe to be the missing person's best interests[88].

s.18 of the Act provides that when determining what is in the missing person's best interests, the guardian must consider all the relevant circumstances of which guardian is aware, and must consider, so far as is reasonably ascertainable, any relevant wishes and feelings expressed by the missing person at any time, including any written statement, the beliefs and values that would be likely to influence the missing person, and any other factors that the missing person would be likely to consider.

Where it is reasonably practicable and appropriate to do so, the guardian must take into account the views of any persons of whom the guardian is aware with a relevant interest in relation to the missing person's property or financial affairs. The consequences of taking a proposed action must also be considered. However, the guardian is not required to decide any matter by reference to the decision the missing person is likely to have taken, or to consider whether or when the missing person might cease to be missing. In relation to this last issue, it is noted that a missing person may cease to be missing within the context of the Act either because they are found, or because circumstances or the passage of time means that it is appropriate for a declaration of presumed death to be made under the Presumption of Death Act 2013.

[88] s.8

If it would be reasonable to expect the missing person to consult a particular person before making a decision, the guardian must consult that person unless it is not reasonably practicable to do so[89]. This could presumably be either a professional such as an accountant or a lawyer, or simply a third party who may have a connection to the issue in question, but who does not fulfil the criteria of having a relevant interest in the missing person's property or financial affairs.

It is expressly stated in the Code that a best interests decision under the Act is to be assessed in light of the provisions of the Act, and it cannot be assumed that the outcome will be the same as a best interests decision made under a different statute, for example the Mental Capacity Act 2005.

Guidance of the Court

If a guardian is unsure as to whether or how to act in a particular situation, or the scope of their authority under the order and the Act, a guardian can apply to the court for directions. Alternatively the court can give such directions without an application[90]. The court can also make a declaration, upon an application or otherwise, that action taken by a guardian was within or outside the scope of the guardian's authority or that a guardian has or has not performed a duty under the order[91]. In the event that a guardian is found to have acted outside the scope of their authority, or failed to perform a duty, the court can sanction the guardian by disallowing expenses which would otherwise be recoverable, or by ordering the guardian to make a payment to the missing person or their estate.

89 s.8(3)

90 s.10

91 s.11

Expenses and Records

A guardian is entitled to be reimbursed from the missing person's estate for reasonable expenses, and the court may direct that a guardian is entitled to remuneration for exercising the functions as a guardian. In return, a guardian must keep records and accounts of their actions, and upon ceasing to be a guardian, must provide a copy to such persons as the court directs[92].

Duration of the Order

A guardian is appointed for the period specified in the order, and there is a maximum period of 4 years beginning with the day upon which the order was made. The court can, however, make a further order in respect of some or all of the missing person's property and/or financial affairs, including an order re-appointing a person as a guardian[93].

For the situation where there is more than one guardian is appointed, see chapter 12, and for revocation of an order see chapter 15.

[92] s.9

[93] s.7

CHAPTER FIFTEEN

VARIATION AND REVOCATION OF AN ORDER

Revocation

A guardianship order is automatically revoked by the death or declaration of presumed death of the missing person, the death of the guardian[94], or the expiry of the guardian's period of appointment[95].

The court may revoke a guardianship order, but only if it is satisfied that

(a) the person to whom the guardianship order relates is no longer missing, or

(b) in all the circumstances, revocation is in the missing person's best interests[96].

Revocation can be made upon application or by the court without an application, but any person applying for revocation must meet the 'sufficient interest' test[97]. For the purposes of an application for

94 Although see chapter 12 for the situation where there are two or more guardians appointed

95 s.14 and see chapter 12 for the situation where there are two or more guardians appointed

96 s.13

97 See s.19 and chapter 11

revocation, the following people are to be treated as having sufficient interest:

(a) the missing person and the missing person's personal representatives;

(b) the missing person's spouse, civil partner, parent, child or sibling;

(c) the guardian.

If a guardian has reason to believe that the missing person is no longer missing, the guardian must apply to the court as soon as reasonably practicable for the revocation of the order, and where a person becomes aware of an automatic revocation due to the death or presumed death of the missing person or guardian, that person must inform the Public Guardian as soon as reasonably practicable[98].

If a guardian acts within the scope of their authority at a time when, unknown to the guardian, the order has been automatically revoked due to the death or presumed death of the missing person, the guardian does not incur any personal liability because of the revocation[99].

s.15(2) provides that if, in ignorance, a person deals with a guardian after the guardianship order has been revoked, the transaction is, in favour of the third party, as valid as if the order had not been revoked.

Where the interest of a purchaser[100] depends upon whether a transaction between a guardian and a third party is valid by virtue of s.15(2), in the following circumstances it is to be conclusively presumed in favour of the purchaser that the third party did not know of the revocation:

---

98 s.14(3)

99 s.15(1)

100 As defined at s.205(1) of the Law of Property Act 1925

either

(a) the transaction between the guardian and the third party was completed within 12 months of the guardianship order being made, or

(b) before, or within three months of completion of the purchase, the third party makes a statutory declaration that they did not know of the revocation.

For the purposes of s.15, knowledge that the order has been revoked includes knowledge of an event which would cause automatic revocation (i.e. death or presumed death of the missing person, or the expiry of the guardianship order).

Variation

The court may make an order varying a guardianship order on, or without, an application being made[101], but any person applying for a variation must meet the 'sufficient interest' test[102]. For the purposes of an application for variation, the following people are to be treated as having sufficient interest:

(a) the missing person's spouse, civil partner, parent, child or sibling;

(b) the guardian.

The court can only vary an order if it is satisfied that

(a) the person to whom the guardianship order relates is missing,

[101] s.12

[102] s.19 and chapter 11

(b) either the absence or urgency condition is met[103], and

(c) in all the circumstances, the proposed variation is in the missing person's best interests[104].

The power to vary an order includes the power to:

(a) appoint a different person to be the guardian;

(b) add or remove property or financial affairs, subject to s.12(4);

(c) add, remove or alter conditions or restrictions;

(d) alter the period for which the guardian is appointed, although not so that the maximum period of 4 years is exceeded;

(e) do anything else that the court could do on making a guardianship order[105].

s.12(4) provides that where the urgency, but not the absence, condition is met, the court can only deal with property or financial affairs in respect of which the urgency condition is met.

Upon making a variation order, the court must send a copy of the order to the Public Guardian.

s.15(2) provides that if, in ignorance, a person deals with a guardian at a time when the guardianship order has been varied, the transaction is, in favour of the third party, as valid as if the order had not been varied.

---

103 s.3 and chapter 12

104 s.12

105 s.12(3)

Where the interest of a purchaser[106] depends upon whether a transaction between a guardian and a third party is valid by virtue of s.15(2), in the following circumstances it is to be conclusively presumed in favour of the purchaser that the third party did not know of the variation:

either

(a) the transaction between the guardian and the third party was completed within 12 months of the guardianship order being made, or

(b) before, or within three months of completion of the purchase, the third party makes a statutory declaration that they did not know of the variation.

106 As defined at s.205(1) of the Law of Property Act 1925

CHAPTER SIXTEEN

APPLYING FOR A GUARDIANSHIP ORDER

Before applying for a guardianship order, an applicant should ensure that they have sufficient interest to make the application[107], that the missing person is missing within the meaning of the Act[108], that the criteria of domicile/habitual residence is satisfied[109] and that thought has been given to the powers sought by the proposed guardian and the proposed scope of the order[110].

Once an applicant is ready to proceed, the claim can be prepared. Applicants should note that the procedure to apply for a guardianship order is very prescriptive and close attention should be paid to the provisions of CPR 57 and Practice Direction 57C.

Proceedings under the Act must be issued in the High Court in either the Chancery Division (now part of the Business and Property Court) or the Family Division, and the Civil Procedure Rules ("CPR") apply to all applications even if brought in the Family Division, save that the provisions of the Family Procedure Rules 2020 relating to the drawing up and serving or orders apply in place of the CPR in Part 40[111]. Applications must be issued using the Part 8 procedure[112].

---

107 See s.19 and chapter 11

108 See s.1 and chapter 11

109 See s.2 and chapter 11

110 See chapter 13

111 CPR 57.26

112 CPR 57.27

Contents of Claim Form and Written Evidence

Because applications under the Act procced under Part 8, particulars of claim are not required. Instead, a claim is issued by the issue of a Part 8 Claim Form (N208) and the claim form must be accompanied by any written evidence upon which the applicant intends to rely.

The claim form for an application under the Act must state:

(a) that Part 8 of the CPR applies to the application,

(b) the question the claimant wants the court to decide, or the remedy being sought and the legal basis for the claim to that remedy,

(c) if the claim is being made under an enactment, what that enactment is, and

(d) if the claimant is claiming in a representative capacity, what that capacity is[113].

In addition, CPR 57.27(3) provides that the claim form must also include,

(1) information about the claimant—

(a) the claimant's name and address, and, if different, their address for service;

(b) the relationship of the claimant to the missing person; and

(c) if the claimant is not the missing person's spouse, civil partner, parent, child or sibling, or other person with

113 CPR 8.2

automatic sufficient interest, details of the claimant's interest in relation to the missing person's property or financial affairs;

(2) the name and last known address of the missing person (who must be named as a defendant), and when and for how long they have been missing;

(3) details of the terms of the guardianship order sought including the name of the proposed guardian;

(4) if applicable, that the claimant seeks a guardianship order on the basis that the urgency condition applies.[114]

The claim form must be accompanied by a witness statement containing the following information[115]:

(1) as far as the claimant knows—

(a) the missing person's name and surname, and any other names by which the missing person is or have formerly been known;

(b) the missing person's gender;

(c) the missing person's maiden surname (if any);

(d) the missing person's date and place of birth;

(e) the occupation of the missing person;

---

114 PD 57C 1.1

115 CPR 57.27(3)

(f) the existence, name and surname, and the current residential or electronic address and any nominated address for service of—

(i) the missing person's spouse or civil partner,

(ii) the missing person's parents;

(iii) the missing person's siblings;

(iv) the missing person's children;

(g) the missing person's National Insurance number;

(h) the missing person's usual place of residence, and when they became absent from it;

(i) the missing person's usual day-to-day activities and when they became absent from them;

(j) whether it is asserted that the missing person is in prison or has been detained, and if so where and from what date;

(k) the date and circumstances in which the missing person is thought to have become missing; and whether there has been any police investigation, and, if so, whether any such report has been or could be obtained;

(l) the missing person's whereabouts, and any evidence or contentions with regard to the matters set out in section 1(2) (the missing person's whereabouts);

(m) any evidence or contentions with regard to the matters set out in section 1(3) (the missing person's ability to make relevant decisions);

(n) reasons for supposing that the missing person is still alive; and

(o) what, if any, steps are proposed with regard to service of the claim upon or other notification of the claim to be given to the missing person, with reasons for such steps being considered appropriate;

(2) reasons why the claimant considers the court has jurisdiction to hear and determine the claim under section 2(2) (applying for a guardianship order);

(3) reasons why the claimant asserts that they satisfy the requirement to have a sufficient interest in relation to the missing person's property or financial affairs, having regard to section 19 (requirement for applicants to have sufficient interest);

(4) if not the claimant, the name and address of the proposed guardian together with evidence that the person consents to acting as guardian;

(5) details of the missing person's property and financial affairs as are known to the claimant and relevant to the claim for a guardianship order;

(6) reasons why, in all the circumstances, the appointment of a guardian in respect of property or financial affairs of the missing person is in the missing person's best interests (sections 3(2)(c) and 18);

(7) an explanation as to why the proposed guardian meets the requirements to act as guardian set out in section 4 (choice of guardian);

(8) details of any persons referred to in rule 57.29(1)(a) to whom the claimant cannot send notice of the claim and reasons for this;

(9) details of the public news media in which the claimant proposes to advertise the claim (rule 57.29(1)(b)) and reasons why it is appropriate;

(10) details of any registered Lasting Power of Attorney or registered Enduring Power of Attorney, or confirmation that no Lasting Power of Attorney or Enduring Power of Attorney has been registered, by or in relation to the missing person; and

(11) details of any Deputy appointed or confirmation that no Deputy has been appointed on behalf of the missing person under the Mental Capacity Act 2005.

If the applicant is relying upon the urgency condition[116], the witness statement must also provide reasons why the claimant considers the urgency condition is met, and attach any evidence which supports this contention.

A guardianship order is a significant order, giving a guardian power over the missing person's property and financial affairs, usually without the knowledge of the missing person. Such applications are also generally unopposed, and therefore the court will want to scrutinise the evidence filed in support to ensure that the information required has been provided and that the procedural requirements have been met. To this end, it is good practice to draft the witness statement using the headings provided in the CPR as this allows the judge to see clearly that the rules have been complied with. This will also prevent delays in the application

---

116 s.3(3) and Chapter 12

being granted as there is a risk that witness statements will be returned to the applicant for re-drafting if the judge has 'find' the necessary evidence.

As an applicant under the Part 8 procedure must file all written evidence intended to be relied upon with the claim form, the witness statement which accompanies the claim form should be as full as possible, covering not only the information set out above, but also any other matters the applicant wishes the court to take into consideration. Any documents relied upon should also be included.

Fitness to Act

It is not a specific requirement under the Act or the CPR to file evidence as to the fitness to act of the proposed guardian, but it is recommended that the application is accompanied by written evidence from an independent third party of good standing stating that the proposed guardian is fit to act, similar to that required for a replacement personal representative[117].

The Missing Person as Defendant

CPR 57.27(4) provides that the missing person must be named as the defendant to the claim, but the claimant need not take any steps to serve the claim form upon the missing person unless the court orders otherwise, which issue will be considered at the first hearing.

If the evidence is such that there is no indication at all as to the likely location of the missing person, then it is likely that service will be dispensed with. It is however feasible that a person can be missing within the definition of the Act but still in sporadic contact with friends or family, for example by email. In these circumstances, consideration

[117] PD57 13.2

should be given at the first hearing to serving the claim form at the email address, along with a method by which the missing person can be served with the evidence in support and draft order upon proof of identity.

Giving Notice of the Claim

Although the claim form and evidence do not need to be served upon the missing person, CPR 57.29 provides that, within 14 days of notification of the date of the first hearing, the claimant must "send notice of the claim or application to those of the following persons whose identity and current residential or e-mail address or nominated address for service are known to the claimant or applicant .... by sending (subject to any redaction ordered by the court...) the material set out in paragraph 3.1 of Practice Direction 57C ...".

PD 57C paragraph 3.1 provides:

> The material required to be sent as notice by rules 57.29 or 57.30 must include (subject to any redactions ordered by the court) a copy of the claim form or application notice, a copy of the evidence in support, and a letter stating the date of the first hearing of the claim or application and that—
>
> "Any spouse, civil partner, parent, child or sibling of the missing person is entitled to intervene in the matter. Any other person having an interest may apply to the court for permission to intervene in the matter.
>
> If you wish to give notice of intention to intervene or to apply to the court for permission to intervene, you should do so at [COURT ADDRESS] as soon as possible, and no later than 14 days before the date of the first hearing, and serve a copy of that notice or application on the [CLAIMANT/APPLICANT] at the address given below. Delay may harm your prospects of obtaining permission to

intervene if you are not entitled to intervene, and in any event, may be taken into account on any question relating to costs."

The persons to be served with the claim form and evidence are:

(i) the missing person's spouse or civil partner, parent, child, and/or sibling

(ii) in the absence of any of the above, the nearest relative of the missing person known to the claimant

(iii) any guardian or any former guardian of the missing person; and

(iv) any person who has previously intervened in and/or become a party to these or any proceedings in which a guardianship order was sought in relation to the missing person.

No later than 7 days before the first hearing, the Claimant must file a witness statement confirming compliance with the notice requirements and attaching a certificate of service in Form N215.

Advertising the Application

Within 14 days of notification of the date of the first hearing, the applicant must advertise the claim in at least one public news media circulating in or relating to the vicinity of the missing person's last known usual place of residence. The advertisement must be in a form which meets the requirements of paragraph 4.1 of PD 57C. The advert can be placed either online or in print[118].

No later than 7 days before the first hearing, the claimant must file a witness statement confirming compliance with the requirement to

[118] Code paragraph 6.28

advertise the claim, and exhibiting evidence of the advertisement along with details of how, where, and when it was advertised[119].

Relief from Sanctions

Under s.20(3) of the Act, if the applicant has not complied with the CPR rules relating to advertising or serving notice of the claim, the court must refuse to hear the application. Therefore, if either of these conditions have not been met, or have not been met within the required time, it will be necessary for the claimant to apply for relief from sanctions.

CPR 3.1(2)(a) provides that the court may extend or shorten the time for compliance with any rule or practice direction, even if the application for extension is made after the time for compliance has ended. As the first hearing of an application under the Act is usually a case management hearing, a failure to comply with s.20 need not be fatal to the application, but in applying for relief from sanctions the claimant should ensure that the witness statement addresses the *Denton*[120] criteria; (i) the seriousness or significance of the breach, (ii) the reasons why the failure or default occurred, and (iii) all the circumstances of the case.

---

119 CPR 57.29(3)

120 Denton v TH White Ltd [2014] EWCA Civ 906

CHAPTER SEVENTEEN

INTERVENORS

Although not named as defendants upon the claim form, the missing person's spouse or civil partner, parent, child, or sibling, may intervene in proceedings for an application for a guardianship order. Any other person wishing to intervene requires permission from the court, and the court can only grant permission if it is satisfied that the proposed intervenor has sufficient interest in relation to the missing person's property or financial affairs[121].

Automatically entitled

Any person who is entitled and wishes to intervene should notify their intention as early as possible, and not later than 14 days before the first hearing, by filing with the court and serving on the claimant, notice in writing specifying:

(1) the intervener's name and address;

(2) their relationship to the missing person;

(3) the reasons for intervening; and

(4) particulars of any determination, order or directions sought[122].

---

121 s.21

122 CPR 57.31

Upon receipt of the notice, the court may give case management directions.

A failure to comply with the rules in relation to applying to intervene shall not prevent a person from intervening, but may be taken into account on any question relating to costs.

The court may direct that a person intervening be added to the proceedings as a claimant (with their permission) or as a defendant.

Requiring Permission

Any person wishing to intervene who requires permission, must file an application in accordance with CPR 23 with the court and serve it upon the claimant as early as possible, but in any event no later than 14 days before the first hearing.

The application must specify:

(1) the applicant's name and address;

(2) why they assert that they have a sufficient interest

(3) their relationship to the missing person or other interest in the proceedings;

(4) the reasons for applying for permission to intervene; and

(5) particulars of any determination, order or directions sought[123].

If the claimant receives an application to intervene from a person who has not been sent the claim form, the claimant must, within 7 days, send the proposed intervenor a copy of the claim form, evidence in support,

[123] CPR 57.31

and notice of the hearing date, and must file with the court and send to the proposed intervenor, a statement setting out whether they object, and any evidence in support of their objection[124].

If permission to intervene is granted, this may be subject to conditions and upon granting permission, the court may give case management directions.

The court may direct that a person intervening be added to the proceedings as a claimant (with their permission) or as a defendant.

---

124 CPR 57.31

CHAPTER EIGHTEEN

HEARINGS AND ORDER

The First Hearing

CPR 57.27(2) provides that, after issue, the court will fix a date for the first hearing of the claim which shall be not less than 56 days after issue, although any person may apply for an earlier hearing date.

At the first hearing the court will consider what directions if any, to make in relation to service of the claim upon the missing person, or whether service should be dispensed with. If the evidence is such that there is no indication at all as to the likely location of the missing person, then it is likely that service will be dispensed with. It is however feasible that a person can be missing within the definition of the Act but still in sporadic contact with friends or family, for example by email. In these circumstances, consideration should be given at the first hearing to serving the claim form at the email address, along with a method by which the missing person can be served with the evidence in support and draft order upon proof of identity.

The court will also use this hearing to check that the formalities of the Act and the CPR have been complied with, deal with any applications for relied from sanctions, and may consider any application for permission to intervene.

Under the Presumption of Death Act 2013, it is mandated that an application "must" be listed for a case management hearing[125]. Notwithstanding the same, the court has held that where all the requisite

[125] PD 57B 1.4

steps have been taken by the claimant, the formalities complied with, and there is no opposition, the application can be heard at the first hearing.

There is no requirement for a case management hearing for a guardianship application which, upon issue, is simply listed for a "first hearing"[126]. There would therefore seem to be no reason why an application cannot be disposed of at the first hearing if all formalities have been complied with, the evidence is complete, and there is no opposition to the same.

The Order

The terms to be included in the order have been considered in chapter 13. Unlike for an order under the Presumption of Death Act 2013, there is not a specific chancery or family form to adapt for a guardianship order. It will therefore fall to the applicant to draft the same. As the guardian gets their authority to act from the order (and the Act), care should be taken to ensure that the order empowers the guardian to carry out the acts required, for example the selling or leasing of property, or the making of gifts to specified people.

If an order is made, the court must send a copy to the Public Guardian[127] but there is no need to serve the missing person unless the court orders otherwise[128]

[126] CPR 57.27(2)

[127] s.3(4)

[128] CPR 57.28(4)

CHAPTER NINETEEN

APPLYING FOR A REVOCATION OR VARIATION ORDER

An application to revoke or vary a guardianship order must be made in accordance with CPR 23[129]. The application notice must also include or be accompanied by a statement containing the following information:

(1) the applicant's name and address;

(2) the applicant's relationship with the missing person;

(3) why the applicant asserts that they satisfy the requirement to have a sufficient interest in relation to the missing person's property or financial affairs,

(4) the reasons for the application and the details of the determination, order or directions sought; and

(5) the persons to or upon whom the applicant proposes to send or serve the application.

(6) as far as the applicant knows, the existence, name, surname and current residential and electronic address, and any nominated address for service, of—

(a) the missing person's spouse or civil partner;

[129] Contrast this to the Presumption of Death Act 2013 which provides that applications for revocation must be brought by issuing a new claim

(b) the missing person's parents;

(c) the missing person's siblings;

(d) the missing person's children;

(e) if there are no persons within sub-paragraphs (a) to (d), the nearest relative of the missing person known to the applicant;

(f) any guardian or any former guardian of the missing person;

(g) any person who has previously intervened in and/or become a party to these or any proceedings in which a guardianship order was sought in relation to the missing person;

(7) what, if anything, is known of the location of the missing person; and

(8) details of:

(a) any persons referred to in rule 57.29(1)(a) to whom the applicant cannot send notice of the application and reasons for this; and

(b) the public news media in which the applicant proposes to advertise the application and reasons why it is appropriate.

Upon issue of the application, the court shall fix a date for the first hearing which shall be not less than 56 days from the date of issue, although any person may apply for an earlier hearing.

Within 14 days of being notified of the date of the first hearing, the applicant must send notice of the application and the material set out below, to the following persons whose identity and address for service are known:

(i) the spouse or civil partner of the missing person;

(ii) any parent of the missing person;

(iii) any child of the missing person;

(iv) any sibling of the missing person;

(v) if there are no persons within paragraphs (i) to (iv), the nearest relative of the missing person known to the applicant;

(vi) any guardian or any former guardian of the missing person;

(vii) any person who has previously intervened in and/or become a party to these or any proceedings in which a guardianship order was sought in relation to the missing person

The material which must be sent is:

(a) a copy of the application notice and the evidence in support,

(b) a letter stating the date of the first hearing of the application, and

(c) a notice in the following terms:

That

"Any spouse, civil partner, parent, child or sibling of the missing person

is entitled to intervene in the matter. Any other person having an interest may apply to the court for permission to intervene in the matter.

> If you wish to give notice of intention to intervene or to apply to the court for permission to intervene, you should do so at [COURT ADDRESS] as soon as possible, and no later than 14 days before the date of the first hearing, and serve a copy of that notice or application on the [CLAIMANT/APPLICANT] at the address given below. Delay may harm your prospects of obtaining permission to intervene if you are not entitled to intervene, and in any event, may be taken into account on any question relating to costs."

The application must also, within 14 days of the applicant being notified of the date of the first hearing, be advertised in at least one public news media circulating in or relating to the vicinity of the last known usual place of residence of the missing person.

No later than 7 days before the first hearing of the application, the applicant must file a witness statement with the court confirming

(i) service of the application upon the persons specified above, and exhibiting certificates of service, and

(ii) the advertisement of the application, and exhibiting evidence of the same including details of how, where, and when it was advertised.

There is no need to serve the application upon the missing person unless the court orders otherwise.

Other Applications under the Act

An application may be made to the court for directions as to whether or how a guardian should act in a particular circumstance, or the scope of their authority[130]. An application can also be made for a declaration that a guardian performed or failed to perform a duty, or that an action taken by a guardian was within or outside the scope of their authority[131].

These applications must be made in accordance with CPR 23. The application notice must also include, or be accompanied by a statement containing the following information[132]:

(1) the applicant's name and address;

(2) the applicant's relationship with the missing person;

(3) why the applicant asserts that they satisfy the requirement to have a sufficient interest in relation to the missing person's property or financial affairs,

(4) the reasons for the application and the details of the determination, order or directions sought; and

(5) the persons to or upon whom the applicant proposes to send or serve the application.

(6) as far as the applicant knows, the existence, name, surname and current residential and electronic address, and any nominated address for service, of—

  (a) the missing person's spouse or civil partner;

  (b) the missing person's parents;

---

130 s.10 and see chapter 14

131 s.11 and see chapter 14

132 PD 57C 2.1

(c) the missing person's siblings;

(d) the missing person's children;

(e) if there are no persons within sub-paragraphs (a) to (d), the nearest relative of the missing person known to the applicant;

(f) any guardian or any former guardian of the missing person;

(g) any person who has previously intervened in and/or become a party to these or any proceedings in which a guardianship order was sought in relation to the missing person;

(7) what, if anything, is known of the location of the missing person; and

(8) details of:

(a) any persons referred to in rule 57.29(1)(a) to whom the applicant cannot send notice of the application and reasons for this; and

(b) the public news media in which the applicant proposes to advertise the application and reasons why it is appropriate.

Upon issue of the application, the court shall fix a date for the first hearing which shall be not less than 56 days from the date of issue, although any person may apply for an earlier hearing.

Unlike applications for an order or a variation/revocation of an order, there is no requirement under s.20 for notice to have been given to specified persons, or the application to have been advertised before the court will hear the application. However, s.20(5) states that rules of court may make provision for service or notice or advertisement, and CPR

57.30 provides that unless the court dispenses with the need for notice, within 14 days of being notified of the date of the first hearing, the applicant must send notice of the application and the material set out below, to the following persons whose identity and address for service are known:

(i) the spouse or civil partner of the missing person;

(ii) any parent of the missing person;

(iii) any child of the missing person;

(iv) any sibling of the missing person;

(v) if there are no persons within paragraphs (i) to (iv), the nearest relative of the missing person known to the applicant;

(vi) any guardian or any former guardian of the missing person;

(vii) any person who has previously intervened in and/or become a party to these or any proceedings in which a guardianship order was sought in relation to the missing person

The material which must be sent is:

(a) a copy of the application notice and the evidence in support,

(b) a letter stating the date of the first hearing of the application, and

(c) a notice in the following terms:

That

"Any spouse, civil partner, parent, child or sibling of the missing person

> is entitled to intervene in the matter. Any other person having an interest may apply to the court for permission to intervene in the matter.
>
> If you wish to give notice of intention to intervene or to apply to the court for permission to intervene, you should do so at [COURT ADDRESS] as soon as possible, and no later than 14 days before the date of the first hearing, and serve a copy of that notice or application on the [CLAIMANT/APPLICANT] at the address given below. Delay may harm your prospects of obtaining permission to intervene if you are not entitled to intervene, and in any event, may be taken into account on any question relating to costs."

No later than 7 days before the first hearing of the application, the applicant must file a witness statement with the court confirming service of the application upon the persons specified above, and exhibiting certificates of service.

There is no requirement for the application to be advertised, but this may be directed by the court[133].

133 CPR 57.30(4)

CHAPTER TWENTY

DWP ORDERS

Practice Direction 6C of the Family Procedure Rules is entitled "Disclosure of Addresses by Government Departments" and applies when the court makes an order, having the power to do so, or makes a request for the purposes of tracing the address of a party or prospective party to family proceedings. The practice direction sets out the information required to be sent to the government department when an order is made by the High Court for the current address of the person named in the order.

It is clear from practice direction 6C and standard order 3.3[134] that the High Court has inherent jurisdiction to order a government department to disclose the current or last known address of a specified person to the court. This can clearly be of assistance in an application for a guardianship order if a person who has been missing for a long time is thought to have had contact with a government department (e.g. had a driving license, paid tax, or was in receipt of state benefits, or payments such as child benefit or a state pension).

An application for a disclosure order against a government department should be made by application at the time the claim is issued, and the order sought can be for disclosure to the court only, or to the applicant's solicitor, upon undertakings by the solicitor not to disclose the

[134] Standard order used in the family courts see https://www.judiciary.uk/guidance-and-resources/update-to-standard-orders/

information or use it for any purpose other than that specified in the order[135].

The CPR does not have a similar practice direction so applications which are likely to be accompanied by a disclosure application can either be issued in the Family Division of the High Court, or the Family Court standard order can be adapted, the applicant having relied upon the inherent jurisdiction of the High Court to make the application.

135 See Standard Order 3.3

MORE BOOKS BY LAW BRIEF PUBLISHING

A selection of our other titles available now:-

'A Practical Guide to Probation Breaches and Other Applications' by Mark Thomas
'A Practical Guide to Remarriage and Divorce' by Cordelia Williams & Claire Howard
'A Practical Guide to Privacy, Transparency, Reporting Restrictions and Closed Proceedings in the Court of Protection' by Laura Mannering
'Beaumont on Barristers – A Guide to Defending Disciplinary Proceedings (Second Edition)' by Marc Beaumont
'A Practical Guide to Payments for Environmental Services' by Ben Sharples
'A Practical Guide to the Law of Pregnancy and Maternity at Work' by Rebecca Thomas
'A Practical Guide to Redundancy – Second Edition' by Philip Hyland & Collette Moore
'A Practical Guide to International Issues for Scottish Family Lawyers' by Susie Mountain, Donna McKay, Ken MacDonald
'A Practical Guide to the Law on Deprivation of Liberty' by Ben Troke
'A Practical Guide to Rights over Airspace and Subsoil – Second Edition' by Daniel Gatty
'A Practical Guide to the Law in Relation to Inquests' by Ramya Nagesh
'A Practical Guide to the Construction and Rectification of Wills and Trust Instruments (Second Edition)' by Edward Hewitt
'A Practical Guide to Data Protection in Social Housing' by Clare Paterson
'A Practical Guide to Spousal Maintenance – Second Edition' by Liz Cowell
'A Practical Guide to International Parental Child Abduction Law (England and Wales)' by Dr Onyója Momoh
'A Practical Guide to Deprivation of British Citizenship' by Sean Ell
'A Practical Guide to Commercial Property Service Charges' by Rachel Garton
'A Practical Guide to Clinical Negligence – Third Edition' by Geoffrey Simpson-Scott (Geoff)
'A Practical Guide to the Rights of Grandparents in Children Proceedings – Second Edition' by Stuart Barlow

'The Electronic Communications Code: A Practical Guide – Second Edition' by Kerry Bretherton KC, James Castle, Mark Loveday
'A Practical Guide to the Independent School Standards – September 2023 Edition' by Sarah McKimm
'A Practical Guide to Estate Administration and Crypto Assets' by Richard Marshall
'A Practical Guide to Parental Alienation in Private and Public Law Children Cases' by Sam King QC & Frankie Shama
'Contested Heritage – Removing Art from Land and Historic Buildings' by Richard Harwood QC, Catherine Dobson, David Sawtell
'The Limits of Separate Legal Personality: When Those Running a Company Can Be Held Personally Liable for Losses Caused to Third Parties Outside of the Company' by Dr Mike Wilkinson
'A Practical Guide to Transgender Law' by Robin Moira White & Nicola Newbegin
'A Practical Guide to 'Stranded Spouses' in Family Law' by Mani Singh Basi
'A Practical Guide to Residential Freehold Conveyancing' by Lorraine Richardson
'A Practical Guide to Pensions on Divorce for Lawyers' by Bryan Scant
'A Practical Guide to Challenging Sham Marriage Allegations in Immigration Law' by Priya Solanki
'A Practical Guide to Digital Communications Evidence in Criminal Law' by Sam Willis
'A Practical Guide to Legal Rights in Scotland' by Sarah-Jane Macdonald
'A Practical Guide to New Build Conveyancing' by Paul Sams & Rebecca East
'A Practical Guide to Inherited Wealth on Divorce' by Hayley Trim
'A Practical Guide to Practice Direction 12J and Domestic Abuse in Private Law Children Proceedings' by Rebecca Cross & Malvika Jaganmohan
'A Practical Guide to Confiscation and Restraint' by Narita Bahra QC, John Carl Townsend, David Winch
'A Practical Guide to the Law of Forests in Scotland' by Philip Buchan
'A Practical Guide to Health and Medical Cases in Immigration Law' by Rebecca Chapman & Miranda Butler
'A Practical Guide to Bad Character Evidence for Criminal Practitioners by Aparna Rao
'A Practical Guide to Extradition Law post-Brexit' by Myles Grandison et al
'A Practical Guide to Hoarding and Mental Health for Housing Lawyers' by Rachel Coyle

'Stephens on Contractual Indemnities' by Richard Stephens
'A Practical Guide to the EU Succession Regulation' by Richard Frimston
'A Practical Guide to Solicitor and Client Costs – Second Edition' by Robin Dunne
'Constructive Dismissal – Practice Pointers and Principles' by Benjimin Burgher
'A Practical Guide to Religion and Belief Discrimination Claims in the Workplace' by Kashif Ali
'A Practical Guide to the Law of Medical Treatment Decisions' by Ben Troke
'Fundamental Dishonesty and QOCS in Personal Injury Proceedings: Law and Practice' by Jake Rowley
'A Practical Guide to the Law in Relation to School Exclusions' by Charlotte Hadfield & Alice de Coverley
'A Practical Guide to Divorce for the Silver Separators' by Karin Walker
'The Right to be Forgotten – The Law and Practical Issues' by Melissa Stock
'A Practical Guide to Planning Law and Rights of Way in National Parks, the Broads and AONBs' by James Maurici QC, James Neill et al
'A Practical Guide to Election Law' by Tom Tabori
'A Practical Guide to the Law in Relation to Surrogacy' by Andrew Powell
'A Practical Guide to Claims Arising from Fatal Accidents – Second Edition' by James Patience
'A Practical Guide to Asbestos Claims' by Jonathan Owen & Gareth McAloon
'A Practical Guide to Stamp Duty Land Tax in England and Northern Ireland' by Suzanne O'Hara
'A Practical Guide to the Law of Farming Partnerships' by Philip Whitcomb
'A Practical Guide to the Law of Unlawful Eviction and Harassment – Second Edition' by Stephanie Lovegrove
'A Practical Guide to Costs in Personal Injury Claims – Second Edition' by Matthew Hoe
'A Practical Guide to the General Data Protection Regulation (GDPR) – Second Edition' by Keith Markham
'A Practical Guide to Working with Litigants in Person and McKenzie Friends in Family Cases' by Stuart Barlow
'Protecting Unregistered Brands: A Practical Guide to the Law of Passing Off' by Lorna Brazell
'A Practical Guide to Secondary Liability and Joint Enterprise Post-Jogee' by Joanne Cecil & James Mehigan

'A Practical Guide to the Pre-Action RTA Claims Protocol for Personal Injury Lawyers' by Antonia Ford
'A Practical Guide to Neighbour Disputes and the Law' by Alexander Walsh
'A Practical Guide to Coercive Control for Legal Practitioners and Victims' by Rachel Horman
'A Practical Guide to the Law of Driverless Cars – Second Edition'
by Alex Glassbrook, Emma Northey & Scarlett Milligan
'A Practical Guide to TOLATA Claims' by Greg Williams
'A Practical Guide to Elderly Law – Second Edition' by Justin Patten
'A Practical Guide to Responding to Housing Disrepair and Unfitness Claims' by Iain Wightwick
'A Practical Guide to the Law of Bullying and Harassment in the Workplace' by Philip Hyland
'How to Be a Freelance Solicitor: A Practical Guide to the SRA-Regulated Freelance Solicitor Model' by Paul Bennett
'A Practical Guide to Prison Injury Claims' by Malcolm Johnson
'A Practical Guide to Advising Clients at the Police Station' by Colin Stephen McKeown-Beaumont
'A Practical Guide to Antisocial Behaviour Injunctions – Second Edition' by Iain Wightwick
'Practical Mediation: A Guide for Mediators, Advocates, Advisers, Lawyers, and Students in Civil, Commercial, Business, Property, Workplace, and Employment Cases' by Jonathan Dingle with John Sephton
'The Mini-Pupillage Workbook' by David Boyle
'A Practical Guide to Crofting Law' by Brian Inkster
'A Practical Guide to the Law of Domain Names and Cybersquatting' by Andrew Clemson
'A Practical Guide to the Law of Gender Pay Gap Reporting' by Harini Iyengar
'NHS Whistleblowing and the Law' by Joseph England
'Employment Law and the Gig Economy' by Nigel Mackay & Annie Powell
'A Practical Guide to Noise Induced Hearing Loss (NIHL) Claims' by Andrew Mckie, Ian Skeate, Gareth McAloon
'An Introduction to Beauty Negligence Claims – A Practical Guide for the Personal Injury Practitioner' by Greg Almond
'Intercompany Agreements for Transfer Pricing Compliance' by Paul Sutton
'Zen and the Art of Mediation' by Martin Plowman
'A Practical Guide to Adoption for Family Lawyers' by Graham Pegg

'A Practical Guide to Industrial Disease Claims' by Andrew Mckie & Ian Skeate

'A Practical Guide to Conducting a Sheriff Court Proof' by Andrew Stevenson

'A Practical Guide to Vicarious Liability' by Mariel Irvine

'A Practical Guide to Applications for Landlord's Consent and Variation of Leases' by Mark Shelton

'A Practical Guide to Relief from Sanctions Post-Mitchell and Denton' by Peter Causton

'A Practical Guide to Equity Release for Advisors' by Paul Sams

'A Practical Guide to Financial Services Claims' by Chris Hegarty

'A Practical Guide to Financial Ombudsman Service Claims' by Adam Temple & Robert Scrivenor

'A Practical Guide to Running Housing Disrepair and Cavity Wall Claims – Second Edition' by Andrew Mckie & Ian Skeate

'A Practical Guide to Holiday Sickness Claims – Second Edition' by Andrew Mckie & Ian Skeate

'Arguments and Tactics for Personal Injury and Clinical Negligence Claims' by Dorian Williams

'A Practical Guide to Drone Law' by Rufus Ballaster, Andrew Firman, Eleanor Clot

'On Experts: CPR35 for Lawyers and Experts' by David Boyle

'An Introduction to Personal Injury Law' by David Boyle

These books and more are available to order online direct from the publisher at www.lawbriefpublishing.com, where you can also read free sample chapters. For any queries, call us on 0844 587 2383 or email us at mail@lawbriefpublishing.com.

Our books are all generally in stock at www.amazon.co.uk with free next day delivery for Prime members, and at good legal bookshops such as Wildy & Sons.

We are regularly launching new books in our series of practical day-to-day practitioners' guides. Visit our website and join our free newsletter to be kept informed and to receive special offers, free chapters, etc.

You can also follow us on Twitter at www.twitter.com/lawbriefpub.

www.ingramcontent.com/pod-product-compliance
Lightning Source LLC
LaVergne TN
LVHW022106200926
848481LV00003B/1073

9781916698673